Real Estate Investing in 2019

Discover How Average Joes Like You are Getting Rich with the Latest Rental Property, Wholesaling, Development, Flipping and Marketing Strategies (Beginners Guide)

Written by Brian Ferrandino

purposes only. All effort has been executed to present accurate, up to date, and reliable, complete information. No warranties of any kind are declared or implied. Readers acknowledge that the author is not engaging in the rendering of legal, financial, medical or professional advice. The content within this book has been derived from various sources. Please consult a licensed professional before attempting any techniques outlined in this book.

By reading this document, the reader agrees that under no circumstances is the author responsible for any losses, direct or indirect, which are incurred as a result of the use of information contained within this document, including, but not limited to, — errors, omissions, or inaccuracies.

Table Of Contents

Introduction

'Money' – this is the only term that we are interested in. Even if you are planning to start a business, or enter real estate, the ultimate reason is to earn money. Only a few people will think about experience, skills, and all that, but the majority will be concerned with making money.

The bitter reality is no matter how much you earn, you still feel as if it is not enough. But, don't worry, you are not alone. We all belong to the same group. Hence, we look for better ways to generate income. You might come across a lot of choices, but deciding the right source of income can be pretty tough.

But the saddest part is most people are interested in one of the successful income-generating paths, i.e., real estate investment. But, their interest doesn't turn into practice. They don't enter the market because they are afraid. Yes, fear is the hurdle they have to surpass.

If you stop thinking and start working, it wouldn't seem as if real estate is hard. You wouldn't fear the market. But how will you begin real estate investing? How will you matter this financial freedom? There can be challenging parts in your journey, but that doesn't mean you cannot achieve success in real estate investment. If you make an effort to understand the market, you will be able to begin your journey as a naïve investor.

Also, remember, every successful investor was once a beginner. If you are a beginner, don't take 'impossible' as an answer. You can also become one of those successful investors if you try a little bit harder.

The real estate investment is lucrative, hence, giving up on it might be an insensible act. Once you read this guide, you will be able to settle for an ideal option. There are wide ranges of real estate investment opportunities in the market. Hence, reading this guide will help you decide your choice.

"Buy real estate in areas where the path exists and buy more real estate where there is no path, but you can create your own." – David Waronker, American real estate investor.

If you want to create your path, if you're going to make passive income, and if you're going to be financially independent, this is your path! However, this book will cover a lot of sections that you will need as a naïve investor, and that includes:

Real Estate Investing for Beginners Like You

Commercial real estate

Rental property investing

Flipping houses

Real estate trading

Wholesaling real estate

REIT investing

The different types of real estate properties

Turnkey

Vacation rental

Multifamily home

Apartment rental

Commercial rental

Making Passive Income

The different ways to make money with real estate

How to turn real estate to a long-term plan

Tips to get good deals when financing

The step of understanding property valuation

Guidelines to decide that you are selecting the right property

Key points to determine a good and a bad deal

Mistakes made by naïve real estate investors

Why should you enter the Real Estate World?

Earning will never be easy if you don't do it in the right way. You will have to show commitment, dedication, and hard work. Meanwhile, guidance to success is a click away. You can purchase this guide to begin your investing journey even with naught experience.

Chapter 1: Real Estate Investing for Beginners Like You

Looking for an opportunity to make money? Of course, there are manifold in the business world that you can try. But no specific business or niche can guarantee a steady income. Why? If you look at the business world, it may look fancy. Businesspeople might be making millions. It took them years of experience, dedication, and hard work to achieve their goals. Oh, wait! Am I discouraging?

If yes, I apologize. The truth has to be said as it is. So far, many people would have plastered it with countless unattainable options, but now, it is high time to see the reality. If you are planning a startup, I guess, it is an excellent decision. Nowadays, more people focus on startups than ever before. But the point is how many of them are successful? Or how many of the startup-oriented people have taken the initiative without being glued to the plan? Well, it is quite questionable. There are great startups, and I'm not pointing at the entire crowd but the majority.

Nevertheless, let's come to you. Do you want to follow the herd? Don't you think there would be better choices than startups? Think!

There is no hard and fast rule for you to follow the herd or to start a startup if you want to make money. Besides, how can you launch a startup while doing your day job? Quite tough, right?

So, think of better options and better methods that you will utilize less time yet make more money.

REAL ESTATE!

Have you ever given a thought about it?

Most people, actually, like real estate, but there is a hurdle that they stumble upon – FEAR! Yes, fear. As humans, we usually fear trying something new. Some exceptional people are ready to take the risk; they don't fear. They have a positive mindset. I think successful businesspeople and investors have such a mentality.

Well, if you don't have an optimistic mindset, you can improve it!

Anyway, back to real estate. Don't you think it is a good option? If you are on the fence, this guide will help you become biased towards real estate.

When you complete this book, you will feel as if you are ready to take up the challenge. But remember, a book cannot teach everything in the real estate world.

Then, what can? EXPERIENCE MY FRIENDS, EXPERIENCE!

This book is for a kick-start, but then, you will learn real estate when you get your hands on the market. Furthermore, as a beginner, there are a lot of things that you must learn. Let me cover a few essential parts.

"Real estate is an imperishable asset, ever

increasing in value. It is the most solid security that human ingenuity has devised. It is the basis of all security and about the only indestructible security." – Russell Sage, American Financier, and Politician.

Hence, starting your journey as a beginner isn't impossible. The simplest definition of real estate is that you invest to make a recurring income that will benefit you in the long run. But, you don't have to believe something that is not true, meaning, if you have heard that real estate doesn't have any expenses someone has deluded you.

Generally, there is no business nor any other income-generating methods that involve no expenses. Thus, when you are investing in real estate, you will come across expenses such as taxes, maintenance costs, insurance charges, and utilities.

Real estate investment becomes pretty simple if the basics of investment are mastered. Factors such as risks, economics, and investment should be understood to perform better in real estate. Through the income that you make from investment, you can target even more properties. Well, real estate investment is simple, but not easy. Hence, the aftereffects of an error can be massive. You might end up becoming bankrupt.

However, as a beginner, you have to gather the knowledge related to making different ways of income in the real estate investment world. So, here are a few income-generating methods:

Ancillary Income – This type of investment income can make a substantial profit. Ancillary income includes a vending machine in a low-rent property. Thus, this kind of income acts like mini-income generating methods in your epic investment journey. Most naïve investors overlook this factor without knowing the importance of it. You have to think out of the framework to find something new and exciting to make ancillary income. It is a matter of creativity!

Cash Flow Income – This is like the main income stream in real estate investment. For example, the rent that you collect from rental building. If you take steps to enhance this income source, you will be able to add storage units, car washes, and much more to this and it will increase the cash flow. But, the most needed factors here are systems placement and management.

Real Estate Appreciation – This income generating method is when the value of the property changes with market fluctuations. There are different reasons for property valuation such as land development, population growth, increase in infrastructure near the property, and much more. You must not forget the fact that real estate appreciation is tricky. Unless you understand it well, you wouldn't be able to make use of it. However, if you make an effort to understand the way it works, it might become your favorite choice. There is something great about this income-generating method, i.e., if you are a smart person, you will be able to analyze the fluctuations and work on it.

Related Income – This is also a possible form of making income in the real estate market. Brokers, agents, and management companies are included in this type of income method. So, agents and brokers' income will be on commissions made by trading properties. But, the real estate management companies gain income from rents. They will receive a percentage of the rent because the management company keeps an eye on the management needs. You don't have to spend too much time to understand this method because it is simple to understand.

So that's about the income-generating methods in the investment industry. However, there are a few tips that every naïve investor needs to know. Here we go:

If you are purchasing real estate investments, there are different ways. It can vary according to the opinions of the buyer, but then, there are specific tips that should be followed. You can use debt to invest in properties. Or you can utilize leverage if you cannot afford otherwise. Anyway, leverage can be dangerous if it is a falling market. You must be careful if you are considering leveraging because payments and interest can drive you crazy to the point where you'd go bankrupt.

You must NEVER buy a property in your name. For risk reasons, you can consider buying properties through different legal entities; limited partnerships or limited liability companies. It is much better to talk to an attorney to understand the suitable method. By consulting an attorney or by purchasing on an entity's name, you will be able to save yourself from unfortunate situations like losing your assets.

Okay, once you've got things right, you can focus on the type of investment that you want to invest in!

So, what are the options that you are left with?

Would you prefer commercial real estate? Rental property investing? Or what about flipping houses?

Wait, you can't conclude without considering the type of investment in detail. Let's begin learning!

Commercial real estate

This specific investment type will top all the other types. There are fundamental indicators that you must consider when you are investing in commercial real estate. The main factor is an exit strategy which is not something essential for wholesales and flips. The commercial property is a kind of land or property that can be leased for retail or business purposes. The categories are industrial, leisure, office, retail, multifamily housing, and healthcare. So, what if you purchase land? If the land has been bought for real property development in any of the above sections, then it can be defined as commercial property estate.

So, commercial real estate is the path to making

passive income and massive wealth. For a naïve investor, commercial real estate offers better advantages than residential investments: lower vacancy risks, steady income, cash flow, and much more. Of course, like everything else even commercial real estate has its cons, however. With due diligence, you can always get what you are seeking. But the important point is understanding the complete picture of the commercial real estate market. Let's go:

Like I already said, this is not similar to residential investment, so the prior purpose is business and leasing out. Usually, properties are office, retail, apartment buildings, and multi-use buildings. Anyway, it is time to learn the ways to get started as a commercial real estate investor. So, shall we?

It's a cut and dry answer – due diligence. No matter the things you do, if you are new to it, you would obviously search, learn, analyze, and then only will you master it. Similarly, if you want to know the ways to invest in commercial real estate, you must learn and analyze. Learning whatever it contains is the key to success. Thus, is this a viable option? Let's see!

1. Comprehend why commercial real estate stands out

If you don't understand that there is a difference in the way of valuing residential and commercial properties, you wouldn't be able to understand the rest. Since the income is based on the utilized square footage, more income can be earned with the use of multi-family houses. Even the lease is longer than for residential properties so you can focus on better cash flow. You must not overlook the location because it is essential. If you find a less demanding location, you would have to struggle with tenant vacancies. Also, you must try to gather information on the neighborhood of the property. By doing so, you would be able to build a good understanding about the neighborhood which is required for a long journey.

2. Inspect comparable

This is important because through this you would be able to understand future developments in the particular area. If you inspect comparable, you would be able to collect the prices of the similar homes that have sold recently. The size, style, and locations will be taken into consideration. Through comparable inspection, you can analyze the present market value.

3. Emphasize on the success metric

These success metrics are used to value the commercial as well as other real estate properties. The problem is you would have to deal with finance and math when you are in the real estate market. If you are great at these, then, no worries. However, be you math-savvy or not, you cannot run away from the commercial real estate formula.

Cap Rate – There will be an absolute value for income generating properties, so this metric is used to find it. This will provide the future estimations on the cash flow.

Net Operating Income – This is used to get the calculation of costs and revenue of a property. Everything put together before taxes and the estimate will help the investors to conclude the expenses and income.

Cash on Cash – The returns that you gain from the transaction can be measured with this metric. This is used when the investors focus on financing (more on this later). This is great because you get the analysis of the cash invested so that the performance can be studied accurately.

That being said, you have to be a market researcher as it is the key to investing paradise. Of course, every beginner struggles with foreign formulas. It will only take a few days to convert foreign formulas into domestic formulas because you will learn the market quickly. Before taking a step, make sure to test the ups and downs in the commercial real estate investment.

Let's start with the positive

Potential earning – We all look for this factor. None would disagree! Well, this is what commercial real estate offers over others. These properties provide a high return based on the location. Usually, it is 6%-12% per annum. Comparatively, it is higher than single-family property return off.

Professionalism – The concern would be on the livelihood, so professionalism would be at its peak. Usually, LLCs handle commercial properties, and they treat this like a business. So, they look forward to building a professional relationship with their customers.

General public – The primary focus of retail tenants would be the general public. It would be impossible for them to grow without the public. Thus, they would do what it takes to make the public happy and satiated. If they neglect, it will backfire on their business. The bottom line is both the owners and the tenants target one thing

– General public. So, the tenants will protect and maintain the property even if they don't want to, that's one of the best things about commercial real estates.

No night shift – You don't have to run if there is an emergency like fire alarms because you have hired a company to take care of emergencies. They will do the needful. And this is not only for fire alarms but also for every emergency. Hence, you are not a 24/7 service provider, and you can focus on your day job!

Easy valuation – You don't have to go through a lot of procedures. Instead, you can quickly evaluate the income statement of the current owner and decide the price. A knowledge broker transaction will involve the investor's earning based on the cap rate of the area. But, it is a different story for residential property. You would have to deal with emotional pricing. Hence, it is easier to evaluate the commercial property.

Flexible lease terms – Lease terms are comparatively flexible. There are countless state laws, termination rules, and security deposits for residential real estate. But, it is not the case with commercial lease terms. So, this is a significant advantage.

Moving on to the negative

Commitment – Of course, this is one of the hardest things in commercial real estate because you must be committed. Despite the number of tenants, you would have more to do than a residential property owner. If you want to maximize ROI, you have to be considerate about being active on the market. When you own a commercial property, you have to do multiple leasing, adjust annual CAM, safety concerns, and much more.

Professional hand – Unless you are a licensed management service provider, it is better not to consider the DIY method. The reality is you would need someone professional to handle maintenance. Of course, there will be a cost, i.e., payment must be paid to the professionals. Thus, you have to include this cost when evaluating property price. However, you must do the evaluation beforehand and make sure to decide whether you are going to outsource or not.

Substantial upfront cost – If you compare two instances such as obtaining a residential and commercial property in the same location, the upfront cost will be higher for the commercial property, so it is pretty tough to become the number one buyer. Even after investing in the property you would have to deal with capital expenditure that is not minor. In a few months, you would have to settle a huge payment for the repair and maintenance of the property. The more customers, the higher the costs.

Higher risks – There is always public visitors for commercial properties; therefore, it is not a shock that there would be a lot of damages. You will have to deal with different types of damage because it is not something that you can control.

However, this is one of the downsides that you have to consider.

That's pretty much it about commercial real estate investment. As a beginner, you would be able to gather a lot of knowledge. But, you have some more choices, shall we have a look at them?

Rental Property Investing

One of the choices that you have is rental property investment. Rental property or, in other words, vacation property is purchased with the intention of a second home and investment. The rental income is charged upon the house to offset the cost. However, before you purchase this kind of investment property, there are a few things that you must consider, for example, the location. As this is a rental property, you would have to think about the popularity of the location. You have to check whether the location has a higher visitor's inflow or not. If there is no popularity you have to deal with vacancy rates, so why all those hassles if you find a good location. You have to focus on things like national parks, beaches, mountains, and so on. Thus, it attracts visitors. Let me mention a few things that you must consider to find the right rental property. Here we go:

Ways to get the right rental property

In the recent past, the popularity of rental properties has parachuted.

Along with the popularity, the options to find a rental property too increased. You can easily find a property online, or with the help of turnkey companies, or even a realtor will help you find a suitable property that has higher ROI. Let's dig into a few ways:

Online Listings – This can be the best option for a naïve investor. If you want to find the right rental property you have to consider online listing because it is beneficial. You can pick a few destinations. Once you have chosen a few locations, you can learn more about local attractions, restaurants, and more. Through this method, you would be able to find the best property that can generate higher ROI.

Get help from a realtor – If the above option helps or not, you better get help from a realtor as well. The realtor will help you view the property. If you get help from a realtor, you would be able to enjoy a lot of benefits. For instance, the realtor will help you understand the comparable properties and the current prices of the properties and the rents to be charged. You can ask referrals to find the right realtor. That's about finding the right property.

Different ways of generating income

Once you find the right property, the next thought that would pop in your mind is how to make income from rental properties. Well, there are a few methods that will provide excellent exposure to the market. Do you want to find out about them? The common ways are hotel programs, VRBO, and Airbnb. So, before you decide the exact income generating method, you have to run a glance at the definition or elaborated information provided.

Generate income from hotel program:

This is one of the options to generate revenue from real estate property. The condotel properties can be purchased if you have enrolled in this program. However, the hotel management company/companies will make use of the management services; thus, you wouldn't be able to manage it on your own. Also, there will be a strict schedule for rental when people rent out the properties. The hotel programs will differ based on the location, service paid, and the unit type. The requirement is that you have to own a rental property while signing up for their rental program. The units of the property will be furnished, cleaned, and ready to use. Hence, the access will be given along with all the amenities. You must not forget that condotels charge higher than regular condos because the guests will be provided with hotel amenities. Then again, you have to deal with higher program fees as well.

Make sure to find more information regarding the hotel program before deciding anything.

Generate income from VRBO:

Vacation Rental by Owner is the standard form of VRBO. This happens in the form of online advertising. The owner of the property will be advertising the property so that travelers who are looking for a property will come across the ads to find the right property and then rent it out. You can either manage your property or hire a manager to handle the daily operations. The difference between VRBO and Airbnb is free structures that you can pick from. There will be a few choices for you to choose from if you focus on Airbnb.

Generate income from Airbnb:

Airbnb helps you to get connected to tourists with the need for hotel accommodation. This platform acts as the middleman to help you rent out the property. You have to add a description under the property by mentioning the number of bathrooms, rooms, and other details. It is much better to include photos of your property so that tourists will be attracted to the property. However, Airbnb will charge a certain amount when a tourist books your hotel. You would have to read and understand the service fee ranges, cancellation policy, and all the other rules.

Factors why and why not buy vacation rental property

You can offset the expenses with the income gained while having a profit as well, but for that, you have to charge a reasonable rent. However, if you are charging for a short-term, rent it should be higher when compared to long-term rentals.

Factors why buy vacation rental property

- This is a form of supplement income.

- Possible to offset vacation and homeownership expenses with rentals.

- Tax deduction benefits.

- Enjoy your property whenever you need.

- High chance for property appreciation.

Factors why not to buy vacation rental property

- You need to bear maintenance, utility bills, and property taxes even if you don't receive rentals.

- If hiring a property manager, you have to pay him/her a fee.

- When there are economic downturns, you will face vacancy rates because people don't travel to save money.

- Inconsistent cash flow.

That being said, it is up to you to decide whether to buy or not! Also, there will be pros and cons for every investment property. The best thing about vacation rental property is that you can enjoy it when you need as I said, it is your second home.

Flipping houses

The next type that you can benefit from is flipping houses. What do you think about this? Well, this is when you purchase a home with significant repairs and issues. You have to focus on the property value. What will be the value of the property after repairing? Will it be more valuable than it was? If, yes, then it is worth repairing. After you fix it, you will be able to make profits out of it if you find the right methods to attract buyers. However, there are two ways of flipping houses:

This is about purchasing a property and then making changes to sell it. Hence, the investor will sell it at a better rate than the rate he or she bought it for.

This is about purchasing a home when there is a rise in the value of the homes. Neither repairs nor updates would be done; the investor will resell it after some time. However, he or she will ensure to make a profit when reselling it.

Let's stick to the first type because there is

nothing much to do with the second type. Here are a few things that you need to understand.

Do you think it is a good investment? Once you read the definitions, you might feel as if it is easy. But, it can create wealth or destroy. So, you have to be careful and considerate. Don't be discouraged; if you can do it in the right way, it can turn out as an excellent investment. You won't need years to create wealth if you master this investment. Sometimes you can be fooled to assume that it is a great deal, but end up purchasing a house with a leaking roof. Hence, this kind of deal may discourage you. The best thing that you can do is to understand the opportunities and obstacles related to flipping houses.

The opportunities in flipping houses
No matter the investment type that you have selected, you don't want to handle losses. You need to reap profits, hence, finding the ideal investment type is crucial. However, without

understanding the opportunities related to flipping houses you cannot decide whether it is good or not! Here are a few opportunities that you might like:

Quick profit – There is a potential to gain quick profit, and this is something obvious when you consider flipping houses. Also, this is the reason why naïve investors are interested in flipping houses. There is a high chance for you to earn a high income in a few months. Thus, you have to be vigilant when purchasing the property.

Experience in construction – When you are dealing with flipping houses you will gain experiences in different fields including constructions. You will be handling remodeling, renovating, and repairing. Hence, you have to make an effort to understand these areas so that you gain construction knowledge. You will know what the costs of the materials are. You will have some understanding of plumbing, and so on. In fact, with time, you will easily spot asbestos and molds as well. This knowledge is beneficial because you can utilize it to find the best budget deals.

Local market understanding – Market research is vital for a successful purchase. The best option is to talk to a professional realtor who will help you understand things better. By doing the market research and talking to the realtor, you would be able to get a good understanding. The styles, designs, and the location will help you make a decision. Hence, market research is essential.

Insights on buyers – Once you set up your property for sale, the buyers' insights can be easily accessed. Once you display the flipped property for sale, you can find out what the buyers are interested in. If you get the insights, you would be able to jot down the likes and dislikes of the buyers. With that, you can adjust it on your next flip.

Budgeting for unpredicted costs – Even though you cannot do anything for unpredicted costs, you will be able to budget for unpredicted costs such as constructions delays, building permits, contractor disputes, and much more. These costs can pop up when you are struggling to sell the property; thus, you will get an idea about the property's unpredictable costs.

Enhance the knowledge in real estate – when you purchase flipping houses, you will eventually end up learning about real estate. The first foreclosure will help you understand different ways of financing that are available. Hence, you will gain the complete real estate knowledge that is needed for an investor to begin the journey.

Connecting with different networks – When focusing on flips, the engagement with different networks will also increase. You will connect with realtors, contractors, insurance brokers, attorneys, and many other essential networks. When you build a good relationship with your network, you will be able to gain benefits in the future. Hence, keep your relationships neat and professional.

The obstacles in flipping houses

Even before I say, you should be aware that there will be obstacles involved in flipping houses. If there are no obstacles, it wouldn't sound real. Well, there is a thin line between a flip and a flop. Thus, a minor error will lead to a considerable loss. Here are some of the obstacles that you need to stay away from:

Unpredicted costs – These costs are beneficial only when you can budget the cost. But if you don't, these costs can become an obstacle. These costs will ruin your entire profit. You have to be vigilant if you don't want unpredicted costs to push you down the drain.

Property taxes – You would have to deal with property taxes once the renovations are completed. This can become a headache if you don't find a buyer as soon as possible. Until you find a buyer, you would have to bear the cost of paying the property taxes.

Property holding costs – Once the renovations

are done, you have to bear the mortgage payments, insurance, and taxes until you sell the property. You will lose a lot from your profit when you pay these charges. Also, the longer you hold the property, the higher the cost. Even the maintenance cost must be added to the list because you cannot stay without maintaining the yard.

Hardships in finding the buyer – Your profit will be based on how fast you see a buyer. The more you delay, the more you lose. You would have to bear the holding cost as I mentioned above, so try to find a buyer using different tips.

Stress – One of the major drawbacks is stress. You would be stressed from the beginning until you sell the property. You might have a hard time finding the property. You will have to deal with contractors, realtors, and buyers and some might be hard to handle. Hence, stress persists throughout.

Before making an informed decision, you have to

focus on both opportunities and obstacles. You have to elaborate on the opportunities to find whether they are profitable. Meanwhile, you have to focus on the impediments to stay away from losses and risks.

With that, I've covered the common types of investments that you can consider in the real estate investment industry. But, you should never rush into decisions as it will lead to massive failures. Even before deciding on a specific investment method, you have to do a bit of research on your own. It is always useful to research, learn, and then decide!

However, I will include some more information that will benefit naïve investors like you. But, you have to keep seeking more knowledge and information.

Chapter 2: Real estate trading

Wholesaling Real Estate

Wholesaling real estate is when a wholesaler sets a distressed property under a certain contract to pass it to some other buyer. The wholesaler wouldn't do the fixing and repairing of the property, rather they advertise the property for buyers by having a profit on the contracted property. Meaning, the price of the property will be higher. This is a short-term strategy, and if naïve investors can understand the basics, it is possible to consider wholesaling real estate. However, some naïve investors struggle to differentiate fix and flip investment and wholesaling. But the key differences are obvious. You can easily differentiate if you pay attention to the information provided. If you don't have lump sum money at hand, you can always pick wholesaling real estate because it is one of the best investment methods that requires affordable cash. You would have to deal with complicated rules and legality. However, if you are interested in wholesaling real estate, you would have to know the steps to obtain it. Thus, here we go:

1. Look for a distressed house or property

There is a reason why you have to look for distressed properties, i.e., you will be able to get the property by paying the market value. Hence, what are distressed properties? Those ruined properties or the ones that owners want to get rid of quickly. Now, do you understand why it is important to target distressed properties? You will be able to find buyers who will purchase the property at the price you set, a higher price than you contracted it for. One of the appealing factors that you must admit is the lower capital. New investors try to find distressed properties using free sources. The experienced investors will focus on other paid sources because they have established themselves in the industry. But that doesn't mean you need to stick to free sources; once you become stable in the investing industry you can opt for paid sources.

2. Discuss, convince, and offer

If you are done with the first step, you will have to think about the owner and the offer. You don't have to struggle to find a property but finding a good deal can be tough. Even if you find one, you must discuss with and convince the owner. If the owner doesn't sign the contract, you won't be able to follow the further steps, so, make him or her sign it for you. This is the primary step of wholesaling; you have to negotiate with the owner to sell it for you. This decides whether you can keep engaging in wholesaling or not. When you are talking to the homeowner, make sure to be polite and delicate as you are not a conventional professional. Your communication must clearly show that you are reliable. You can follow three tips to ensure that you communicate well; being courteous, on-time, and professional. If you are done with convincing, you can move on to the offer. At this stage, you have to explain the reason and the benefits why you are the right choice. You can even mention that there wouldn't be any upfront cost for the owner. Also, don't forget to emphasize the repairs so that the owner will accept a fair price.

3. All about the appraiser, contractor, and title companies

An appraiser, contractor, and a title company are needed on your team to complete the procedures. With the help of these professionals, you would be able to complete the procedures smoothly and safely. Each party will impact on your money and time positively if you are planning to do wholesaling long-term. If you work with an appraiser, he or she will provide an appraisal on the desired property at short notice. The appraisal will ensure the price and the profit that you would be making from the desired property. As you are naïve, I'm advising you to see the desired property before you purchase it. Next, the contractor will witness the property to provide an estimate on the repairs to be made. Of course, this doesn't concern you, but it will help you decide the price and the buyer. Lastly, the title company will make sure that the property is legitimate. The company will do a quick check to find whether liens are on the property. Make sure to find an investor-friendly title company. You can find these three important parties with the help of referrals, online, and through recommendations.

4. Evaluate the renovation needs

You will have a profit plan, so by evaluating the property needs, you can find the costs and check whether it fits your plan. If the property needs renovations, it means the investor will gain a higher margin. When you are handling buyers, you can provide the cost estimates prepared by the contractor. The evaluation is a great help when you are negotiating the price. If you know the costs and the property's needs, you will be able to find the ARV pretty easily.

5. Looking for a buyer

You have picked a distressed property, talked

with the owner, had your team, and got the contract signed. What now? It is time to look for a buyer. You will have to deal with a contractor or an investor, but not home buyers because they won't focus on repairing a property. Hence, you have a target market. Based on the settlement date, you must quicken the step of finding the buyer. As a beginner, you wouldn't have a buyers' list, but when you get along with the market, you can prepare a list. Once you advertise your first wholesaling property, you will be contacted by the buyers so, at that time, you have to make a list. When you are preparing the list, you must include contact info, name, and the interest. If you create a spreadsheet with the details collected, you will be able to make use of it in the future. If you have this list, you can save your costs and increase profit.

6. Manage the deal

If you have found a buyer, you have to manage the deal by discussing. This is an important step because it decides whether you make a profit or loss. You have to be vigilant and delicate because he or she is your buyer, in other words, the customer. The amount that you keep when wholesaling is the profit that you make from the desired property. Thus, when you are talking to the buyer, show the estimate provided by the contractor so that it will benefit you. Also, hint on the fact that some other interested buyers are highly interested in this valuable property. During the negotiation, you have to cover all the costs incurred.

7. The closing step

The closing step will happen at the office of the title company, and it will only take 90 minutes. All the related parties will be presented. And then, the current owner will receive the deed. With that, the deal closes, and it is marked completed. The closing date can be seen on both the contractors with the buyer and the owner.

So, that's it about wholesaling real estate. As a naïve investor, you might like this, if you do, make sure to learn more about it.

Is wholesaling right for you?

This is indeed a fantastic question that we must ask ourselves before we step into something new. Even in wholesaling, it is the same question that you must ask yourself. Well, let me help you. There are certain types of people who might be the right fit for wholesaling. Some of them are the ones who don't have enough finance to manage the real estate investing opportunities so that they can consider this option. Or if you are interested in distressed properties and you believe that you can negotiate people, you too can consider wholesaling. Of course, sometimes, you might need a lot of dedication to the work, yet once it reaps out rewards, you will be glad that you picked this investment method.

But, it is better to be prepared by doing some homework as a naïve investor. You can get advice from professionals and investor groups. You have to dedicate time to find the right property and, along with that, become familiar with contracts and agreements.

There are grey areas that you might have to learn and understand. All you need are commitment, confidence, and consistency!

This is one of the methods that is famous and beneficial. Even naïve investors get attracted to real estate trading. What is real estate trading? Are you aware? Also if you are not, you can learn it with the help of this guide. This is an arrangement that requires the seller to sell the property while purchasing a property from the one to whom you are offering it. In simple words, this is the simultaneous-sale approach. Right after the point of deterioration of the real estate market, real estate trading came into the picture. However, in order, make this trading approach work, both the seller and the buyer should have similar demands. Hence, trading properties via this method will increase profit along with tax benefits. Due to the 1031 exchange loophole, you would be able to avoid capital gain taxes.

Also, you would have to focus on other details such as potential profit and risks. The greatest fear or the uncertainty in real estate trading is not being able to manage costs on the property that you are planning to buy after selling your property. Traders must be hawk-eyed on finances as they have to cover every expense including mortgage payments when they are selling a property. Plus, these expenses will be borne without knowing whether they will make a profit or not!

You must always focus on the property value that you are planning to exchange because there is no point in selling and transferring properties without a profit. Or you can trade inexpensive properties that have lower maintenance costs.

The "I-buy-yours-you-buy-mine" trading agreement is something different, yet profitable. There are differences when compared to the traditional. To start with, exchanging land titles, settling netted differences, no lump sum upfront payment, and many other factors. A person with negative equity property cannot take part in the trade based on the financial capacity.

Online trading is an excellent method to reach the market as a naïve investor. You can easily profit if you market the properties in the right manner. Also, make use of the internet aptly. If you do so, the payback will be huge. For example, if you are marketing a particular property, you can post pictures of the property on websites that catch the eyes of the ones who want to engage in trading. It is a matter of commitment and hard work.

There's more, shall we keep reading?

REIT investing

REIT or Real Estate Investment Trusts means the investment equities. These are used to boost portfolios. There will be higher dividend returns and risks. Before you think about REITs, you must know what it is and how it is done and all the other details. Well, REITs are companies that own and handle real estate properties. Familiar

REIT companies may engage in purchasing and managing apartments. Also, there might be companies that invest in commercial or some other properties, so, they are specific about their investment type. According to the law, 90% of profits should be dividend distribution. Certain REITs have the quarterly distribution method for profits; thus, it becomes a significant income source for retirees. REITs do not have to handle corporate tax. As a beginner, specific details may sound harsh to understand, but through research, you can learn more about it.

Do you like REIT investment? Or do you want to give it a try? If yes, keep reading, if not, skip to the next chapter. However, there are different REITs such as mutual funds, exchange-traded funds, and closed-end funds. You will come across popular ETFs such as iShares Cohen & Steers Realty (ICF), Vanguard REIT Index ETF (VNQ), SPDR Dow Jones REIT (RWR), and much more.

You can create a brokerage account if you want to

purchase individual REITs without any middlemen. There are REITs such as Equity Residential (EQR), Ventas (VTR), Public Storage (PSA), and many more individual REITs that you can consider. As you are new to the investing world, I recommend working with a professional who is well-versed in REITs.

Thanks to the investors, they have found a lot of methods to connect with REITs overseas markets. Well, it can be risky as you are a beginner; then again, as recommended, join up with a professional. By investing in Overseas REITs, you will be able to gain higher yields and diversification.

You might feel good to invest in REITs, but do you just make decisions without even considering the pros and cons? Let me help you by mentioning the pros and cons.

Pros and cons related to REITs investment

You already know that the REITs investment is popular. Most investors who are experienced will prefer REITs, but an inexperienced investor will think twice. Well, you don't have to think twice. Instead focus on the pros and cons of REITs investment. If you are aware of the pros and cons, you will be able to make the right decision. The assets in the REITs companies are mostly real estate holdings. Most REITs are equity or mortgage REITs. Most REITs investment properties are office, industrial, retail, and other types. Anyway, here are pros and cons of REITs.

Pros and cons factors of REITs

Pros-

- The requirement to pay 90% of net income as dividends.

- Easy sales and purchases.

- Professional management is offered.

- Predictable dividends and cash flow.

- Less volatile prices.

- A wide range of choices.

- Helps to diversify investment.

Cons-

- The requirement to pay 90% of net income as dividends (of course, it is both a positive and a negative factor)

- Dividend taxed like comprehensive income.

- Must pay taxes.

- Highly leveraged.

- Risks in concentrating.

- Rising interest rates.

If you compare REITs to stocks, you will understand the benefits of considering REITs. You must spend the time to elaborate upon each of these pros and cons. Once you do, you will be able to get a better grip on the REITs investment.

Anyway, before moving on with REITs, it is advisable to read, research, and repeat the procedure until you become well-versed with the REITs investment.

Chapter 3: The different types of real estate properties

Now that you have learned real estate trading, it is time to learn the types of properties in the real estate sector. Well, as you already know this is not a small market, rather this is a broad market that consists of a lot of choices. And this is a beneficial sector, but that doesn't mean you can make profits if you are not cautious. When you are making a decision, you have to consider all the possible aspects of real estate trading. A buyer, an owner, or an investor, all must have an understanding of the type of investment. They should understand the significant difference in the types of properties. Since you are a beginner, you wouldn't have the experience, so learning the types of properties in detail is essential. If you have an understanding of the kinds of investments, you would be able to select the ideal investment as per your needs. However, in general, you must learn about the residential property, vacant land, and commercial property. Once you learn them, let's move to a few more specific properties. Here we go:

Residential property – This is a popular type that you must be well-versed in. There are variant types such as villas, apartments, duplexes, and much more. As a naïve realtor, it is essential to know the kind that you have selected. You have to choose the buyer by considering the needs of the buyer and matching it with the specifications of the property. Hence, sales will be smooth and easy.

Vacant land – This is for people with an interest in ranch business. As a realtor, you must know the details of the land that you are marketing. Also, you must research the buyers to make sure that his needs and your offerings equalize.

Commercial properties – If you want to select commercial properties, you have to remain in the market for some time to gain experience because without experience commercial real estate investment will be pretty tough. Both land and building with the commercial purpose can be treated as commercial properties.

These are the major categories that you need to know about. Now, let's learn a few types of investment.

Turnkey

Turnkey investment trading is an exciting type of trading because you would be able to trade from afar. This is the specialty in turnkey investment. You can make passive income in different ways, but this is something out of the box because you gain rentals without actually being there on the property. This means "turn the key." It might sound amazing. But, you shouldn't directly enter the market without learning it. The turnkey market is about the outside local market; you would be exposed to a wider range of opportunities. If you do not know the definition and other details, the turnkey investment may look scary. But, once you learn the details, you can easily master the investment method. The definition in detail:

The definition is flexible and simple because it is "turn-key." The definition means you will be purchasing a property that you have no attachment to or involvement in. Hence, there are different terms such as:

A company will manage the fixed property, so your role is to invest and receive income concerning profits.

OR

You invest in a property that needs to be fixed up. You will be even ready to fix up the property and find tenants, yet, you chose to hire a management service provider to do the needful. On the other hand, you will be collecting income without becoming involved in management activities. Despite your choice, there are two components such as:

- You do not necessarily have to buy local property. You will be exerting minimal effort for a readily available property because that is what turnkey means.

- Purchase property from anywhere, i.e., a lot of opportunities.

Benefits and downside in detail

There are more properties that you can pick from. If you look outside the market, you will find a whole lot of areas and properties that you can utilize to make money. But the problem is rental homes have to be controlled from afar, this can be quiet tough. However, you can hire a management company or a manager to do it for you.

Passive income is another reason why people love to enter turnkey investment. Purchasing and managing properties is not a part-time gig, so time is essential. Hence, turnkey investment is an excellent option because you do not have to dedicate your time. You can focus on turkey investment along with your day job. The income you make will increase, while you will have to offer a little effort to maintain the property. But, you might have to pay a certain amount to the property manager, this can be a drawback if the payment is high.

Lastly, the best thing about turnkey is you would be spending a very low amount to own the property while gaining better income through it. You can get the service from the turnkey real estate company. They will buy, clean, and then sell the house to you. However, they will be charging an amount from you which is their income.

Even though there are certain drawbacks in turnkey investments, it is beneficial. But, don't conclude until you do your research.

Information on Turnkey Real Estate company

This is a company that works to help the realtor

and investors to get hold of the ideal property that they look for. But, they are not the ordinary real estate company because they deal with turnkey investors alone. If you find a property with the help of this company, you will be able to gather all the essential information to make a decision. Also, they have a perfect market understanding.

Risks involved in Turnkey Investments

There are always risks involved in investment properties. Even with turnkey, it is the same story. So, let's get to know some risks:

The vacancy rate of renters – This can be a critical issue when handling a turnkey investment. Your property will remain vacant for some time. So, the strategy to own a few houses rather than sticking to one will be a great choice. If you have one vacant property, you can gain support from other properties. But, if you have one property and if it faces the vacancy rate, you will be doomed.

Third party management – many beginners prefer turnkey because it doesn't require full-time attention, but then, you have to hire a third party to do the needful. It is beneficial if the third party is reliable. If not, it can become a threat to your investment journey. The management company should keep the property or properties safe and clean. So, you have to hire a reliable company.

Not without witnessing it – You will be purchasing the property without observing it; hence, it can be pretty dangerous. You might be tricked into acquiring a property that it is not as worthy as sellers painted it to be.

Not for everyone – Even though beginners can consider turnkey investment, it might not be the right decision for some investors. Also, it is okay since everything doesn't suit everyone. If you don't have the finance or skills that are required to invest in turnkey investment, you can opt for other options.

So, that is it about turnkey investment, and you shouldn't make a decision unless you understand the complete picture.

Vacation rental

In chapter 1, I explained vacation rental properties in detail. So, now, let me mention a few tips that you have to bear in mind when investing in the vacation rental. Shall we have a look at a few tips?

Vacation Rental is like the two-in-one benefit because you own a second home that generates income when you are not using it. The best thing about a vacation rental is you will be able to earn profits and offset it to the ownership cost. When you manage your second home with a business touch, you will be able to create a steady income. However, certain factors make the rental ownership a lucrative business. Of course, location is essential; meanwhile, there are many more factors that must be considered as well.

Your primary goal must be to provide convenience, comfort, and ease to the travelers. In other words, you must make them feel at home. If you do so, it will be easy to find more clients as previous clients will leave positive ratings on the websites where your property is displayed. The effectiveness of word of mouth marketing has not gone out of the market, so you can still hope for it to work for you. So, here are some of the tips you can consider to make your investment worthwhile.

Display the vacation property in a readily available way – The rental property must be in a state of accommodating right away. If you look at specific properties, you will quickly understand that the properties are not taken care of because of minimal management. A house with a hard mattress, TV with unentertaining channels, and other negative factors can shoo away people from considering your property. Hence, even if you have to spend some dollars initially, it is better to set up your rental vacation in an attractive way.

For example, you can decorate the house, add Netflix, and much more. Also, if you include these things you may charge higher rentals as well.

Emphasize on the features – If you can increase the revenue by giving an extra touch to the outdoor space, why not give it a try? Even a lounge chair that provides the statement look to the balcony will attract buyers because they can sit on the chair while enjoying the unsettling ocean. This is why views and locations are outstanding. Or you can place some potted plants to transform the look of the living area of your vacation rental; this will eventually allure the guests.

Focus on exceeding expectations – Not only in the investment sector, but also in every work that you engage in, you must strive hard to provide more than expectations. As the owner, you do not have to break your bank to make the property appealing to the owners. Small details have the power to satisfy guests. For example, if you have setup Netflix, make sure to check whether it is working and the guests can enjoy it without any hassles. Likewise, you have to be considerate about the tiny details that have a higher impact on satisfaction.

Everything next, cleanliness first – Do you agree? This also applies to your life as much as it does to rental property investment. Some rentals fail to achieve this factor. But, if you don't want to lose clients, make sure to keep the property clean. It is very much recommended to hire a professional cleaner if you have money, but if you don't have enough cash, you can do it on your own. When doing it on your own make sure to pay attention to clean every place. With proper cleaning, you can make the place look extra beautiful.

Offer different types of reservations – If you offer different types of reservations, more clients will prefer reserving your property. You can enhance the property by adding bunk beds, sleeper sofa, and more things. With these additions, your property will be rented out sooner.

The ultimate success is when you are excited to stay in your vacation rental. If you are excited, think about the guests? Your main focus should be to connect with the guests so that they rehire your property. If you make it a pleasant stay to one client, he or she will recommend the property to another person. And that's how you connect with a wide range of clients.

Multifamily home

This is not similar to a single-family property; instead you would need a particular investment that suits multifamily property. As a beginner, you wouldn't understand the ways to find the right lender. But, with this guide, you can get some understanding about the multifamily home. The whole process will take three weeks or less if you are aware of the process. There are many lenders that offer loans for this kind of property so you can get their help. You can be prequalified quickly with the support of lenders. However, if you follow these steps, you would be able to invest in the multifamily home pretty quickly.

1. Make sure to do proper research on neighborhoods

Before you step into the multifamily investment, you have to look for a good neighborhood. Even though you might not be residing in the neighborhood, you will have to focus on the tenants' preferences; the units will be rented out sooner. First of all, shortlist some neighborhoods with multifamily homes and bring down the list to one by researching the neighborhoods. The factors that you must consider are:

- Public parks must be considered because tenants need to relax.

- Poor school ratings will deter tenants.

- Attractions such as shopping malls, restaurants, and hotels must be nearby.

- Thriving business sector should be present.

- Walkable space adds the score to the

property.

- Public transportation should be accessible so that tenants get easy access to all the necessities.

- Other properties around the multifamily home should be in a good state, if not it will deter tenants.

- Well-maintained areas will be considered.

So, this is all about finding a good neighborhood that would increase the value of the multifamily home. You can research with the help of the internet, an agent, or by actually witnessing the neighborhood. I advise doing all three so that you collect a lot of knowledge about the neighborhood. You must not invest money on a property that loses its value later on because of the location. Hence, when selecting a multifamily home, you must be mindful about the location and the neighborhood.

2. Select the lender and sign the pre-approval letter

Once you have chosen the neighborhood, you have to focus on the lender and the letter. There are lenders for multifamily loans, and if you find the right lender, you can get things done quickly. They will offer quality customer services as well. And then, you will be provided with a pre-approval letter. Anyway, how will you select the lender? Let me help:

Select the lender – the best choice is an online search. As this is a wide niche, you must look for someone with specialized skills. The lender should offer a great guide on multifamily financing. As you will be receiving investment property loans, you don't have to live there. However, a lender finances a property with 2-4 units. Here are the criterions to adhere to when selecting a lender:

- Compare and contrast the rates of a lender with some other lenders to decide on the ideal one.

- Make sure to check the areas covered.

- If you are in need of rehab loans, make sure to talk to the lender to check whether he or she offers it. Certain lenders don't provide rehab loans.

- Be focused about the payment terms because short-term loans will take up to 3 years and long-term loans will drag on for 30 years.

- Customer service is crucial. You have to look on the lender's website to check the response time and the customer service satisfaction. Also, check the contact details.

Although it's more difficult to find, you may be able to work with a lender through a referral from a local real estate agent, another real estate investor, or from your bank or credit union. For more information on where to find a multifamily loan, how to apply, and what types of loans are offered, check out our guide to investment property loans, guide to multifamily financing, and our in-depth FHA multifamily loan article.

Get the pre-approval Letter – If you have found the lender, the next thing is the pre-approval letter. You have to provide preliminary financial details to the lender so you will be prequalified. The pre-approval letter will include the qualified amount and interest, and the lender will offer it to you. This letter is a requirement that is created to begin their collaboration. This letter will provide support when you handle the agent.

3. Time to get help from an agent

Even if you do your research, you will need the agent's support to walk the rest of the multifamily home investment journey. An agent will help to choose a multifamily home and even negotiate the needful requirements. Most agents who with deal multifamily properties can be found on MLS, i.e., Multiple Listing Service. If you have the support of a real estate agent, you will be able to get things done more comfortably than doing them on your own. It is better to find an agent who has experience in multifamily investment. This is crucial because only through experience will the agent be able to decide the right property. A few things to consider when hiring a multifamily property agent:

- An agent should be available to work with you; if he or she already has a lot of clients to handle, it is not wise for you to hire that agent.

- The agent should specialize in the relevant sector as there are different sectors in the real estate investment.

- The location of the agent's office should be close to the property that you are planning to buy so that he or she can keep an eye on the neighborhood.

- Lastly, that one factor that you cannot

overlook is experience.

So, before you select an agent make sure to increase your knowledge in asking the right questions and other details.

4. Come down to one choice

Once you are done with all the above steps, you have to decide on the multifamily property to be purchased. Well, step 1 and your budget will eventually narrow down the choices to one particular property. However, make sure to look for a property that will offer positive cash-flow. Some of the things that you must consider:

- A Rent-ready property will have a lot of things to be done, so make sure to write down the time, work, and money that you will require to do the needful.

- Focus on the rent roll because it helps to decide the amount that you must charge your tenants.

- You have to decide the carrying costs by considering the vacancy rate per unit for a certain period.

- Lastly, you must calculate the income and expenses to check whether there is positive cash-flow.

With all these factors in mind, you will be able to find a suitable property that can generate good income. However, you must be mindful about the red flags; missing paperwork, unwritten leases, and much more. As a naïve investor, these factors must be your primary concern because you don't want to fall into the pit when you are beginning your journey.

5. Create an offer for the selected property

If you have settled on a property, it is time to create an offer. At this point, the pre-approval letter will be needed with the deposit and your agent will carry out the transaction. There must be an appraisal for the agreed amount. This step is crucial to ensure your honesty and to get back the money deposited.

6. Finalizing and closing the deal

After step 5, you have to finalize and close the deal. The lender will approve the loans after completing the paperwork and other essential requirements. The agent will decide the closing date by considering everyone's convenience. Once the documents are signed, you will get the keys to the property.

Apartment Rental

What about apartment rental? How well are you aware of it? Do you think it is profitable? Well, let's check out the detailed information on the apartment rental along with pros and cons to get the best out of it. Who doesn't like an additional income? Nowadays, people don't stick to one income source, rather they look for a few sources. So, apartment rental is an option to make additional income.

Of course, collecting a steady income from

apartment investment is a great idea. There is high demand for apartments, that means a higher opportunity to make a steady income. People prefer relocating to a place near their workplace. So, you have to be considerate about the location of the apartment that you are planning to invest in. Also, if you have a day job, you can hire a company that manages day-to-day operations. You must consider the costs, time, and your energy when you decide the price. Once you are through with all these details, take a look at the pros and cons.

Apartment Rental Benefits

The significant benefits of apartment rental are that you can enjoy tax benefits. Expenses such as insurance, property management, advertising, and much more can be written off, so it decreases the taxable income. Along with that, you utilize the profit from selling the apartment when purchasing more investments; thus, by putting off capital gains, you can recapture taxes.

The apartment value can be written off each year as depreciation. As naïve investors, these things may confuse you, but make sure to learn more about depreciation if you want to enjoy more benefits.

The best thing of all is you will be enjoying positive cash-flow along with market appreciation over time.

But you shouldn't get carried away just by reading the pro factors. Instead make sure to consider the risks as well.

Apartment Rental Risks

If you think logically, you will understand that there is no risk-free investment method in the real estate investment industry. Each investment method will have its risks and apartment rentals is no different. Here we go with some of the risks involved:

Most naïve investors face the issue of finding tenants, but let's say you found tenants, then, what else can be risky? Sometimes tenants might lose their job, go bankrupt, and many other unavoidable issues can come up when handling apartment rentals.

Or you might rent out the unit to a family with kids, and the family damage the apartment units. This can be a huge cost because you have to renovate or repair to rent it out to another tenant.

Having the ownership is not the cure-all solution. You might face higher tax costs when you make payments for the property.

Also, you'll need money for unprepared expenses and vacancies. There will be fixed monthly costs as well.

Bear in mind, even if there is a manager to take control of everything, your attention and time are needed as well.

Anyway, decision making is not a minor step; you have to think thrice, analyze, and then, finalize the decision. The type of investment that you want to make is also not a minor decision, so even though we have provided some information you have to spend time on research. The more you research, the more you get to know about the investment type. Hence, spend time learning!

Commercial Rental

The commercial rental property has been covered in chapter 1. So, you can understand the definition and other necessary details from chapter 1. In this section, I will mention a few tips that a beginner will essentially require. You may have talked to an experienced investor, and they too would have shared their experienced, but how can it be a guarantee that you will experience similar things on this journey? You wouldn't get the experience, but you can learn from their stories. But you don't feel the pain until you get it. Similarly, you have to try investing in commercial rental to know what it is. You can still target success by feeding your mind with relevant tips, points, and ideas. Here we go:

1. You must invest without collecting

What is the reason for investing in commercial rental property? Simply, you want to earn an income. But will there be an income if you purchase a property that doesn't generate profit? No! It will be collecting properties rather than investing. Hence, when you are buying an investment property, you must focus on certain factors to decide whether it is an excellent property that will generate income. There are many sources from which you can learn the ways to identify the right property to be purchased. So, before you buy a property, you must do some research, browse the market, and compare the pros and cons to finalize the property that you are going to buy.

2. Have plans for upkeep

Not being ready for the future shows that you are not prepared to become a full-time investor. Even if you are a part-time investor, you must have a plan.

"A goal without a plan is just a wish." — Antoine de Saint-Exupéry.

So, you decide whether real estate investment is a wish or a goal!

Coming to the point, at the beginning of the purchase you wouldn't have to bear a cost for maintenance, but with time you will have to bear maintenance costs. No matter the type of property, there will be wear and tear expenses. Hence, the owners have to be prepared for it. Sometimes, certain buildings will upgrade and so on. Especially, commercial properties undergo a lot of damages, more so than residential properties. This is why you need to have a plan!

3. One at a time

Doing everything together can create a huge mess if you are not experienced in what you are doing. Similarly, you have entered the real estate market as a newbie, so if you try to invest in all the types of investment at once, it can become a mess. When you are handling commercial real estate investment, you have to pay undivided attention so that you can find a great property.

4. Focus on the environment

When you are the owner of the commercial property, you will have to cover up the hazardous waste. Of course, you might not be the reason, yet the responsibility delegates over to you. Thus, be prepared for it!

5. Hire a mentor

You can always hire a mentor; don't think twice when you need a mentor. Even though it might cost you some money, they will guide you when needed. By hiring a mentor, you can always push yourself away from mistakes. When you are a beginner in the real estate market you will have to deal with stress, so even in such a situation, they can help you sort the problem and help you to relax.

6. Protect yourself claims

There can be problems and complaints because it

is inevitable sometimes. If you don't want to end up bankrupt, you have to hire an attorney or be in touch with an attorney when making investment-related decisions. Even better, talk to the attorney and make sure that you have covered the legalities in the right manner.

7.   Maintain good bonds

You must feel free to connect with lenders and investors in the real estate investment sector. They will become essential parties when you are investing in the commercial rental, so neglecting or ignoring them is not a good idea. At a point in your investment journey, you might get the chance to buy a million-dollar property. At that time, if you cannot do it alone, you can partner with an investor if you have maintained a good bond. Plus, it is good to know your partner rather than partnering with a stranger.

These tips will help you improve step-by-step, but not immediately. You must know that overnight success is nothing but magic. You can't create magic in the real estate investment market. You can only generate income even it is through hard work, perseverance, and dedication!

Chapter 4: Making Passive Income

Now, it is time to have a look at the popular topic that rules the real estate investment industry. Is it possible to make passive income in the real estate investment industry? Why do some regard it as a myth? Before you conclude, let me tell you one thing: you should never follow the herd. If you believe real estate is worth a try and if you have done enough research on it, you must give it a go because it is worth it. You can gain success if you are persistent.

However, passive income means regular income by doing little to nothing from your end. This means you wouldn't have to exert a special effort to make a steady income. Even if you don't engage in management, you will be paid monthly, quarterly, or annually. But then again, as a naïve investor, you would believe that passive income is a cakewalk. Yet, it is not!

If you want to make it a passive income source, you have to work for it (this doesn't mean you have to be involved in management; instead you have to educate yourself).

Some investments can be utilized to get passive income completely, but then, certain passive income will be less than the others. Likewise, there can be minor differences in the level of income, but that doesn't mean passive income is a myth. But, how will you make income through investing?

Well, there are two methods that you can consider: direct purchase and indirect investment. You wouldn't have the complete control over the property if it is an indirect investment. But then, direct purchase would offer higher returns at the cost of higher upfront payment. So, you can involve in indirect investment through tax alien or REITs investment; these investments don't include direct ownership.

I don't want you to get trapped in this broad market, so you can utilize my advice and tips to build your path in the real estate investment to make passive income.

Can you make passive income through direct investment?

You would have heard people speak about flipping houses. Of course, they are highly profitable, but they are not passive. So, you have to stick to real estate rentals. There is a wide range of real estate rentals, thus passive income earning will differ according to the strategy that you use. You can easily find investors who do very little and gain a lot. If you study their past, you will understand that they have worked to create a profitable path, and now they have established a good source of income so that they can outsource their work while enjoying the profits.

This is an interpretation of passive income. But, the assumption of most naïve investors is completely contrasting compared to this. If you understand real estate investment in the right manner, you will be able to make passive income by hiring out certain parts of the investment process. You will have to bear a specific cost, but you will be generating enough income.

Before you move on with real estate investing, you have to decide. You have to talk to yourself and understand the goal. You must know how much time you are ready to allocate to investing. You need to think about whether you like it. Once you find the answers, you can research and learn about it. Most of the time, real estate involves a lot of learning.

There is no point in having a lesser amount by working hard. You must learn to be realistic. You must focus on the steps that you can actually do, and then you must outsource the other work. There are different methods to hire out; you must research it if you really want to give it a go.

Specific crowdfunding platforms are ideal for

almost everyone. You must learn and find out a lot of things about these platform before you sign up. So, why did I mention this? Well, crowdfunding is one of the popular passive income sources. With the help of crowdfunding, naïve investors will be able to access projects that might benefit them. There are websites that you can consider reliable. As the properties are well-managed, you don't have to think about receiving a call at 2am from the tenant. Crowdfunding management fees will be less than REITs investment management fees.

You can even access a wide range of properties. Because of the extensive exposure to the broader market, you will be able to diversify the risks in the investment and enjoy excellent returns if done correctly.

Well, there are a lot of things that you can learn about passive income making in the real estate sector. But to put it in the simplest form, you have to understand the definition of passive income. You have to make an effort to find the right method to earn passive income. Again, don't follow the herd, but have your path that is created from hard work and dedication. Anyway, if you are not a fan of passive income, you can consider other income methods. I'll mention a few possible ways to make money in real estate investment.

The different ways to make money with real estate

You already know about passive income, i.e., buy-and-hold investments. And the next is active income that you gain from flipping contracts, renovating, and much more. As a beginner, learning all these methods can be daunting, but you must acquire one at a time. You can use this guide to understand the basics of investing so each income generating method will be explained in brief. If you want to learn more, you can always use search engines.

Almost everyone is interested in real estate investment, but only a few are taking the step to learn and understand the market. And, you should be glad because you are reading this guide. If you are reading this guide, you have taken the initiative to your investment plan. Anyway, how does this work? So far, you have learned that income generated income from the real estate investments should exceed the expenses; this means beneficial cash flow. So, this is possible through both commercial and residential rentals and works for long-term and short-term investments. According to studies, apart from business owners, investors make a higher income. However, it depends on the individual. Yet, investing in real estate is one of the wise decision that you can make if you can handle it throughout.

So, there are many income generating sources that a naïve investor can consider when he or she has entered the market. Ah, and, the type of investment, whether it is passive, will differ according to the investment strategy that you utilize. Hence, the following income generating methods will be in general.

1. Residential rentals

No matter the blog or book you read on this topic, you will find essential rentals on the list. A popular way of generating income is through leveraging long-term properties, i.e., residential properties. The simple fact is people will need shelter. They will never say no to a house because it is crucial. Based on that simple fact, you can invest in rental properties. But, investing blindly in some random properties will not be beneficial, so you have to focus on the significant principle: location!

Even in this guide, I've highlighted the importance of location. And you might have heard the same advice from many successful investors. Yet, it should never bore you because it is crucial (here, I'm repeating it!). The location is vital for property value appreciation with time, but it is not the only important thing. You can easily find tenants if the location is excellent.

Plus, this is going to be a long-term gig so don't make silly mistakes and fall into permanent troubles. Any investment in a great location will be advantageous.

The traditional approach is utilized when making through rental properties. You will have to settle a down payment to enjoy the property on a long-term basis. Based on the personal financial situation, you have to decide on the property that you are going to buy making a down payment.

If you are enjoying beneficial cash flow, then you have achieved it. You have made a significant investment. But, if you are not enjoying useful cash flow, you have to liquidate the property to get some cash.

2. Property-renovating flips

If you are assuming that fix-and-flip will benefit you, the time has long gone. Along with the renovation shows that boomed in the industry, people are interested in renovation flip. There is an excellent chance for higher returns, yet it will be based on the knowledge and skill of the investors. As a beginner, you must test the waters before you try swimming. Similarly, as a naïve investor, you must test the market little by little to master it. Hence, if you have no experience and knowledge, there are chances for you to fall into the trap.

There have been successful investors who have tried flipping houses along with renovation. The successful investor Matt Larson advised to pick ugly homes with great neighborhoods. This is where the value gets created. However, if you don't have a good bond with agents and if you don't understand the repair value, you wouldn't be able to achieve success by property-renovation flips.

You have to focus on the value of the home once you have repaired and fixed it. If you want to do this successfully, you must build a link with the contractor and witness the actual property by visiting the site. If you are buying an unseen property, it is highly possible you will lose everything you invested.

If you understand the costs and the potential gain, you will be able to make money by property-renovation flip because it is more straightforward than any other investment method. You must not try to get involved in renovations that you cannot manage. Importantly, you must think of creative ways to change the look of the home. Also, don't forget to make every renovation flip a cost-effective one so that you don't have to handle higher costs. This is one of the income generating methods that you can consider in the real estate market.

3. Lease options

When you lease with the buy option there is no requirement for significant capital or credit. Thus, this is considered a significant income source. This is ideal when the market is on the rise because the pre-set price can come in handy later on. For example, in a rising market, you purchase a discounted property. Then, you can sell the rights of the purchase to another person. This is the bull market situation in the real estate industry (if you aren't familiar with the bull market, you can learn it through research). This is an option, so there is nothing like the set rules to purchase. It is no wonder that you might find it a bit tough because a beginner will need some time to adapt to the market, but over time, you will be well-versed.

4. Short sales

The short sale is when the owner has to deal with the delayed mortgage, yet the property is not on foreclosure. If this type of transaction happens, the parties involved in the transaction must agree on the terms and conditions because the offer price is lower than the current mortgage. You can make a quick profit from this income generating method as it doesn't involve lengthy procedures for renovations. Almost all the default auctions are tricky. You would have to pay the entire amount in cash and certain transactions occur without seeing the actual site. But, the short sale is much better compared to auction as it offers a chance to witness the house before the transaction takes place.

If you are experienced in real estate investing, no worries, but then, if you are a beginner, you have to do a complete inspection and review before taking the risk. This type of income making takes time, but it is worth the time. Returns from short sales are immediate. As soon as the transaction takes place, the materialization happens because the bank wants to get rid of the property. However, you should negotiate a fair price.

5. Commercial real estate

The significant opportunity that you can utilize in the real estate sector is investing in commercial property. You would be able to gain higher ROI if you have selected the right property. Well, developers in the real estate sector focus on developing properties, flipping properties, renovating and upgrading properties, and also adding value. Well, this is a great source to make a steady income as long as the investor adds great importance to the property to gain higher income. The need for a physical location to run a business has been outnumbered, so there is no way that it is going to lose its demand. If you invest in commercial real estate and strive hard to succeed, you are going to win! You have to start to move forward in the real estate sector.

6. Vacation rentals

This is a great path to make a profit in this investment market. You could make a side-income by investing in vacation rentals if you selected the right property. Also, you can turn this into a passive income source if you find a property in a location where there'd be a high inflow of tourists. If there is a high inflow of tourists, it is evident that there will be high demand for vacation rentals.

7. Contract flipping

One of the ways to generate income is through flipping contracts, so you do not need a credit or a higher capital. Both highly motivated buyer and a highly distressed seller are enough to make this work. Of course, you have to try a little harder to find a distressed seller. The hardest part of flipping is the difficulty in finding the parties that I mentioned above. You enter into the contract when you bring these two parties together. However, even in this income-generating method, you will face risky situations that you have to handle carefully.

8. Hard-money lending

Another source of income is hard-money lending. These lenders help the ones who cannot gain loans otherwise. Thus, if you want to turn into a lender, you must have some capital with you. These loans charge a higher interest as they are for short-term periods. This shouldn't be a main income-generating source. But, you can consider this method if you want to enhance your path. You must consider hard-money lending when you have to, a particular position in real estate investment. Even if you don't have significant capital, you can do this with a certain amount of capital as there will be higher returns. The interest rate is high, but it is reasonable. If you become a professional lender, you will be able to make a decent amount of income.

Anyway, there are many more income-generating methods that you can consider if you are in the real estate market, so you don't have to be discouraged if these options don't appeal to you. But it is highly unlikely for you to avoid the above income-generating methods.

Chapter 5: How to turn real estate into a long-term plan

If you want to enter the real estate market, you can easily do it because there are no barriers to entry. Joining is not the challenge, but surviving is! If you want to remain in the real estate market, you must have patience. Without it, you will struggle to continue your journey. Anyway, if you have a long-term goal, i.e., to remain in the real estate market, you have to learn a few things. What are the essential factors that you must master? How should you plan?

Let me tell you; you wouldn't be able to turn your journey into a long-term one unless you have a plan. For example, if you have entered the market with the hype that is created by other investors, it doesn't mean that you have a long-term plan. So, then, what is a long-term plan? You must enter the market by learning it. If you are not ready to be committed, then what is the point in turning your real estate journey into a long-term plan? Before you think about setting your real estate plan to a long-term one, you must check whether you are ready to dedicate your time and attention to real estate investment.

Well, to survive for a long time in this market, you must have a PLAN! So, let me help you with some of the tips that you must utilize when turning your real estate journey into a long-term plan. Here we go:

Be specific about the goals

There are different styles of investing in the real estate investment market. You will come across wholesale, turnkey, and fix and flip investing. The real estate investment market is not a simple market, so you have to specify your goals to stay on track. Even if you come across a myriad of challenges, you will be able to remain firm if you have a specific goal. Anyway, it is essential to understand both specific and non-specific goal. So, here we go:

The particular objective is when you set a

milestone with a timeline. You aim to achieve it within a specified period.

But on the other hand, the non-specific goal is when you set goals without any directions. Hence, you are not aware of the methods to make money. If you don't want to face such problems, be specific with the goals.

Measurable goals are important

Just having an intention to make money will not suffice. Anyone can dream about making money, but not everyone succeeds in it. Well, you don't invest with the aim of losing. So, if your intention is not to lose money, you must have measurable goals. You can easily confuse measurable and immeasurable goals, so let me make it easy for you.

The measurable goal means when an investor plans to purchase a property that offers 6% or more annual rate of interest. Well, if you have a quantifiable goal, things may seem simple. And it is why I recommend you have measurable goals.

On the contrary, if you have a goal to become the top investor in the real estate field, it shows that you haven't measured the purpose. Hence, having a measurable goal will help you stay on track. Put simply, you wouldn't be able to meet the purpose if you have not set measured goals.

Let it be attainable

The goals should be reachable. You should not fall into the trap of greed as the human mind can easily be lured to earn more money in a short time. When you become greedy, you don't think about planning or setting goals. You focus on earning. Unfortunately, if you are grasping to make money, you wouldn't be worried about the plans, and it will lead you to lose rather than gain. The importance of planning is not only for naïve investors but also for experienced investors.

The attainable goal means knowing that the goal is attainable or practical. For example, if you want to invest in a property that offers favorable cash flow, it shows that you are looking for something reasonable. As an investor, you have the liberty to choose what you purchase so it is under your control and it is attainable. But then, if it is a goal to make a considerable profit, say, $150,000 from the initial deal, it is unattainable and impractical. You are a beginner, so as a beginner, can you even think of it? I don't mean to discourage you. I'm practical. When you become experienced in investing you will be able to have such goals. Even then, you have to make sure you consider many other factors to support your goal. In order to turn your short-term plan into a long-term project you must focus on the possible goals. If not you might struggle to remain in the market.

Goals must be realistic

Having realistic goals is essential. Can you become a billionaire right after joining this investment world? Some investors want to earn regular income without a break, but is it a realistic goal? Well, it is not. You are a human.

You need a break. Or if you want to make more income, you must find partners for the real estate deals and divide the profit amongst them. But when selecting partners make sure to find the best ones. Or you can look for some other practical ideas through which you can earn a higher income. However, make sure to differentiate realistic and unrealistic goals.

The realistic goal is when you try to maximize profits with the help of a good property management company. You will be able to make a positive income even if you have to allocate a certain amount for day-to-day operations. But then, the unrealistic goal is when you try to manage the investment property while doing a day job. You must know that it is impossible because there will be a lot of management duties. You cannot do it while having a day job because it is essential to maintain the property to rent it out to tenants.

If you are trying to manage the property without outside support, understand that it is unrealistic.

When you are playing a role in the investment market, you must make sure you set realistic goals while focusing on the resources and other relevant factors.

Learn to set timed goals

Time, this is an important point. Every second is valuable. As a real estate investor, you must know the value of time; you are setting deadlines for you, not anyone else. Hence, you have the opportunity to fix it methodically.

The timed goal is when you set a goal with a deadline. For example, you can set monthly quotas or certain milestones to reach, which means the goal is timed. On the other hand, the untimed goal is when you set a goal without mentioning a period or a particular milestone.

Hence, setting timed-goal is essential. If you are hoping to turn your journey into a long-term plan, you have to bear in mind the planning tips. The crucial part of planning is setting a goal, so with the help of the above points, you will be able to create the right goals. That's pretty much about deciding the plan that you must create. If you don't have a good plan, you cannot turn your investment journey into a long-term one. Anyway, even if you have a plan, you might face challenges because it is the nature of the market. Of course, you can study the market, but that doesn't mean you can predict it 24/7. There will be sudden changes in interest rates, market fluctuations, and much more. So, you have to be prepared for the challenges that you might come across in the real estate investment industry.

However, there is more to goal-setting of importance to be considered. Before you set a goal or before you plan your long-term investment plan you must make sure to consider the following points. Of course, these points may seem simple, but you are not going to achieve it unless you are dedicated. So, shall we have a look at the primary aspects of goal-setting? Here we go:

Goal setting should be systematic. The long-term

achievement cannot be attained just within a short period. You have to be patient while exerting a lot of effort to set the path for success. A goal itself is a system that helps you to reach the success of investing. However, being neglectful when setting a goal is the primary failure. Call to mind, if you are planning to set a goal, it means you have taken the step to achieve the success in your investing journey. There are many investors out there who don't even think of planning their journey. Hence, it is not going to be a good start for long-term success.

With small beginnings comes success; this is true in the real estate. When you enter the real estate investment world, you wouldn't have had a massive plan, or you wouldn't have understood the market. But with time, you would have mastered the way you invest and the way you differentiate good and bad deals. This is what learning means. This is how every journey begins. If you ask an experienced investor the answer will be to start small and achieve big. You don't have to target a significant amount in your first deal because it is impossible. You just have to look for a few properties that suit your budget and financial status. Also, bear in mind, you must not become a debtor to invest in the real estate properties, rather you can have a look at chapter 6 as it discusses financing. You might find some help to finance your investment property.

Don't waste time finding good deals without knowing what good deals are. If you are through with the concept of real estate investment, finding good deals, agents, and all the others would be more straightforward. It is not like you can learn everything related to real estate investment in a day. But, knowing the concept will keep you off the challenges and pitfalls in the real estate investment. Also, remember, you must be up-to-date with the market knowledge if you want to become a successful investor. Even if you are not interested in learning the current market standard, economic status, and all the other important factors, you must learn somehow.

Without this knowledge, you wouldn't be able to manage yourself as a naïve investor. And, this will help you to set high goals.

This is a very competitive platform where you will find many competitors. To compete with them you should know the market well, but how can you compete with them when you don't have the market knowledge? You will be dealing with a lot of people, for example, agents, contractors, and many more. If you don't have the adequate market knowledge, it won't take long to be fooled by others in the market. Also, this is a competitive platform, meaning you cannot move forward if you don't get things right. To get things right, you must set your goals with the knowledge of the competitive market.

Now or never, don't delay because the real estate investment world is filled with many opportunities and competitors too. Hence, if you miss the chance, it might never come. Don't keep wondering about the future, so it is advisable to start it today. You can directly buy a place which wouldn't cost much and then according to a plan renovate it, add fittings, make it look different, then when the time arrives sell it by keeping a profit to cover the expenses. Of course, you have to search for the right property by doing a few types of research. But thanks to the internet, you can easily access the website to find the right property that needs to be purchased. If you start the real estate journey once the thought popped up, you will be able to secure it for a long time. The reason is if you start you can easily continue, and eventually you will find yourself involved in this investment world. So whatever the decisions, make it smart by not delaying or waiting for the opportunity because the opportunities are to be created by you.

Emotions, sometimes, can be your worst enemy. But don't allow them to overpower you. As this is a business platform, you may be defeated sometimes with a considerable loss but thinking about it over and over won't provide any solutions. Instead take it is a challenge and try correcting the mistake and start all over. I know the beginning is always hard. But if you have the spirit to do something you shouldn't think of challenges, risks, and drawbacks. You must focus on the primary goal.

Finally, it is in your hand to turn your investment journey into a long-term plan. No matter how many tips you read and ideas you get, nothing would be beneficial if you don't try it. In the beginning, a long-term plan may seem like an impossible milestone, but with dedication anything is possible. If you believe in yourself and if you learn the market, you can turn real estate investment into a long-term journey. Stop thinking and go for it!

Chapter 6: Tips to get good deals when financing

Most people are aware that real estate is a significant investment. If you can understand the basics of the investment, there is nothing much that you need to understand. If you consider property investment, it has been a great choice of investment for a long time. Also, there are many reasons why people still love to engage in property investment. As naïve investors, it might take some time to understand all these details. Yet, by now you have gathered enough knowledge on investment. However, there is something that you need to learn, i.e., financing. You might struggle to find traditional financing as well because it is quite complicated for a naïve investor.

Well, if you are struggling with the financing, you are not alone because there are many naïve investors out there with the same problem. The best thing about investment is you can easily find a lot of other methods to finance your property. You can quickly get hold of the investment property that you want to if you know a few easy financing methods. It is actually possible to get a good deal when financing, you just have to know a few things. I will help you by mentioning a few financing methods that are ideal for a naïve investor.

Most naïve investors are already in the market, but they are lost in between. They have no idea of the ways to begin their journey. They don't know the simple methods to finance their investment. If you read the following tips that I have provided, you will be able to understand the right type of loan that you must pick as a beginner. Let's begin!

1. By making a down payment

If you prefer a conventional loan, you have to ensure that a certain amount is available at hand for down payment. If you have a sizable amount you can get the best interest rates, so focus on the down payment amount. As a beginner, you will have to adhere to specific strict rules, but over time, you will get better opportunities and advantages. Anyway, the bank may require a down payment of 20% or more on the value of the property because you are a naïve investor. Yet, if it doesn't sound right, no worries. There are many more options for you.

2. Focus on down debt

The DTI means debt-to-income ratio must be taken into consideration. This is another way the bank will assess the ability. The bank will decide whether you can or cannot make monthly payments if they approve the loan. How will you find the DTI? You have to divide the monthly recurring debt by monthly gross income, and then the final amount will be in percentage. And that's what the bank is concerned about.

If you have increased DTI, it means you already have a lot to settle, and it wouldn't be a favorable situation. An increased DTI will not provide the chance to enjoy interest rates. Sometimes, you might even struggle to get finance from other sources.

3. The Good credit score

You must begin this step by checking the credit score. If you are getting the loan from a bank, you will have to deal with credit scores because it will have a significant impact. The terms and conditions of the loan will have a direct effect on the credit score. If you want to get low-interest rates your credit score must be high. Or if you're going to enjoy low-interest rates, you would have to pay a certain fee to the bank. You must be diligent when handling credit scores. You need to have a good credit score. In order to have a good credit score, you must keep an eye on it on a regular basis. You must make payments right on time. You must deal with discrepancies and errors at the earliest. You must not over-utilize if you want to enjoy a high credit score. Also, your credit card limit balance should be 30% or lower and it should be maintained throughout.

Likewise, work on the above factors if you want to enjoy low-interest rates and get easy financing.

4. Fixed-rate mortgage

You will always have two options such as fixed-rate mortgage and an adjustable-rate mortgage. If you pick the fixed-rate mortgage, there will be a fixed interest rate until you settle the loan. But, if you select the adjustable-rate mortgage, you will have to deal with fluctuations, and it can be tough. Homebuyers get attracted to ARMs because of the introductory rates. Although the initial rate would be lower to attract people, it may increase over time. If you pick FRM, you wouldn't have to worry about fluctuations. Or if you are still interested in ARM, it is better to understand the terms and conditions before obtaining it.

5. Have the paperwork

You will need the paperwork despite the lender that you are going to get the loan from. You will be required to prepare essential documents. You will have to submit bank statements (2 months) and CPA letters if you are freelancing or self-employed. Sometimes you might need the statements of the retirement account, driver's license, and divorce paper if there is any, and much more. However, the lender will request a few documents at the time of discussion, so be ready to submit those.

With the help of these tips, you can manage a lot of things when obtaining a loan for your property. But, there are different financing methods that I'll mention below. You might find a few common financing methods whereas, if I miss out any, you must do your research and learn them. Also, don't stick to one source; you must dig in for information as much as you can. Anyway, let's keep reading!

1. Owner occupant method

This is a common method that you would have come across if you have been reading or talking about financing real estate properties. This is about becoming the owner-occupant. You will be purchasing the property for your needs as well as to generate income. So, if you consider the loans provided by the bank, the down payment will be lower when you obtain an owner-occupant loan. Also, it is less than the down payment required for an investors' loan. Sometimes, you will get the chance to enjoy a lower interest rate too. However, you must not forget to check the rules related to this type of loan. Certain banks want you to live in the property for some time. Whereas some other banks do not have this rule. It is better to check the rules and regulations to be in the safe zone.

2. Home equity option

You have a home and equity, you can consider this financing method. You may utilize the equity to finance your property. HELOC, or home equity line of credit, is pretty easy to obtain. And you don't have to undergo all the hassles that you would otherwise face. In fact, you might get the opportunity to obtain 80%-90% of the total equity of the home. This is similar to obtain a regular mortgage. The bank will consider the credit score to ensure that the income that you gain is enough to return the loan. You must not forget the fact that you are using home's equity. This means it is the security for the loan that you have obtained. There are chances for you to lose your property, so it is better to talk to a consultant before making a decision. A professional will provide tips to make the right decision.

3. Property exchange option

You can exchange the home that you already have with the property that you are planning to invest in. When exchanging it, you must look for a buyer who is concerned about your investment goals. If the buyer is concerned about your goals, he or she will help in achieving it. For example, the buyer will be a better rental, help you to purchase the investment property that you need, and so on.

4. Cash-out finance proceeds

Another method of financing is to consider refinancing to get money, and then utilizing it to purchase the investment property. The lower the interest rate, the higher the feasibility. Also, the home equity will impact heavily on this financing method. But, as there is high demand for home values, there are no issues in having high hopes.

5. Subject-To Financing

This means the loan will not be under your name rather it will be under the seller's name. But the title will be yours. But, then you must make the payments. If you don't pay, you will not get the property and the seller will be affected with a bad credit score. This is considered by most naïve investors as there is no requirement for down payment. This is sometimes applied during pre-foreclosure as it offers the chance to the buyers to close the deal as soon as possible. This kind of financing is quite tricky, so you have to be careful.

6. Seller's mortgage assumption

This is more like a subject-to financing. The only difference is the assumption of the buyer about the liability of the deed. If the default payments are on, there wouldn't be any responsibility on the seller. This financing can be utilized during foreclosure at times. In such instance, the homeowner can be tricked easily, and the buyer gets the benefits.

7. Seller's Financing

If there is a property owned by a seller, you can purchase it via owner-financing. In this situation, the seller becomes the bank. The seller provides the title to you, but then have the deed. The monthly payments will be made in exchange for this transaction. The foreclosure can happen if you don't pay. But the problem is it is not easy to find a seller who agrees to this method of financing. But, some sellers prefer this method. But, you will be charged higher interest rates.

8. Lease-to-buy

This is another method of financing. This is great for naïve buyers when they are not familiar with the market. By using this option, you can rent the investment property for a certain time duration. Generally, for 2-3 years before getting the mortgage. The best thing about this financing is that you can secure financing or improve the credit score over time. However, you must make sure to hire an attorney before you sign the agreement without focusing on the terms and conditions.

9. 203K loan

This loan is ideal if you are purchasing a property that requires repairing. This loan will finance the property along with the cost, just 3.5% of down payment. However, to get this loan, you must be an owner occupant. Also, you must occupy it for some time.

10. Self-Directed IRA

If you have this, you would be able to get money to purchase the property without involving stiff penalties. If you handle properly, the expenses and income will automatically be directed to the relevant account through IRA. However, it is better to talk to a financial adviser before making a decision.

11. Self-Directed 401k

This is also similar to the above option. You wouldn't be charged penalties for obtaining the money. Yet, it is better to talk to the financial adviser.

12. Private Funding

This is more like hard-money loans. But, the difference is this has the relationship based feature. You will receive money from a friend, family, or someone you know. This person will be ready to get the investment property. However, there wouldn't be any formalities when you are dealing with private funding. Even the interest would be lower, like 6%-12%.

13. Investment Partner

Another method to get finance is to pair up with a partner. The private lender gets the interest for the money and proceeds will be shared with the equity partner. This can be a 50:50 partnership. But, it is up to you to decide the percentage based on your preference. Based on the income method, the generated income must be divided amongst the partners. It is better to have an attorney so that things can be sorted nicely and smoothly.

14. Turnkey Provider option

This is new, yet gaining enough popularity. If you contact a turnkey company, you will be able to invest in a property that is already rented and managed. This can be considered great if you are investing from afar. Also, some companies offer very low down payments for properties. But, if there is a low down payment, the interest must be high.

15. Local Bank

This is a good option if you shop around. There

might be a lot of requirements from a certain bank, but why stop there? You can go to another bank. If you consider obtaining the loan from a smaller bank rather than considering a large bank, you will be able to enjoy flexibility along with many other benefits. The bank might help to get the finance because their motivation would satisfy the customers. It is better to contact the mortgage brokers as well. Because they will know a lot of loan products. You might get the right fit with their help. You must research before settling for an option.

There I ended the long list of financing options. Some financing options would have been appealing whereas some others wouldn't have been. But, you should bear in mind, despite the financing option that you select you to have to make sure to focus on the pros and cons and other details. If you try to learn the pros and cons before settling for an option, you will be able to understand whether it is a good option or not. Most options that are great for naïve investors might not be right for you, and it is not wrong! You may have different reasons and choices.

But when you are financing the property, you have to think about the type of investment as well. The kind of investment that you have picked will have a more significant impact on the financing option. Anyway, do your duty. Research more on the financing option that you select before deciding.

Chapter 7: The step of understanding property valuation

Do you think understanding property valuation is essential for your investment journey? Well, as I said before, you must have complete knowledge about the market. If you don't have the full market knowledge, you will struggle when you face challenges. If you don't want to get caught in challenges, you must be aware of all the possible aspects of the investment sector. Hence, knowing the method of property valuation is also one of the critical things that you need to be aware of. Actually, we can easily say property valuation, but a property valuer must do a lot to provide a valuation. Can you benefit from this valuations process? Well, you might have a lot of questions right now. You already know that the valuation of the property is an essential part of the investment and it's critical for the investor to understand the complete picture of property valuation. Now, let's dive right into the content.

Do you know what property valuation means? Well, it means the market value that is estimated as per date that the property is being evaluated. This will be based on normal situations when neither buyer nor seller is handling undue pressure. As mentioned in the previous chapters, the valuation will be done by a professional valuer. There is no part in the property for a professional valuer, and the valuation will be valid just for three months. As an investor, you must know the difference between market appraisal and formal valuation. So, what is the difference? The agent prepares the market appraisal whereas the professional valuer does formal valuation.

A professional valuer must have the training and the education, more on this later. The appraisal contains the information that can be considered a guide. This will include information based on recent sales and local knowledge. However, there are different valuations such as Kerbside valuation and Desktop valuation. Kerbside valuation means without any internal inspection done on the property. And Desktop valuation is done with the help of a computer. However, let's stick to full-valuation. This means there will be full valuation along with internal inspection. So. Let's go.

Who is benefitting from valuations? The lenders are the ones who benefit the most from valuations. They need this valuation to find the asset value that is used for security when obtaining loans. And based on it, the lending will be calculated. Even the property owners, buyers, and seller may need a valuation to decide the existing property value or the value of the property that they are planning to acquire. Now, let's move on to the inspection process, how does it happen?

For example, if the inspection has to be made for a house to get a loan:

- Before the approval and finalization

steps of the loan, it is a must for the lender to request a valuation. The valuation can be requested from the independent valuation company that is picked from the valuers' panel.

- And then, the valuer must visit the property to inspect both internal and external. The valuer can take pictures while questioning the homeowner about the property.

- Next, valuation of the land's components will take place so that he can decide the proportion of total value of the property.

- Along with other things, size, aspect, topography, and shape will be assessed.

- During the inspection of the internal property, the size of the property, number of rooms, types of rooms, condition and age of the property, fittings and fixtures, unique characters, and design layouts will be taken into consideration.

- The prospective buyer and the valuer consider almost the same thing when assessing the purchase.

However, the home buyers play a massive role in the investment market and this is why they have a higher impact on the market value. Most of the time, the valuers work under the instructions of a lender. For example, even if the property has the potential to be considered a triplex or duplex, if the lender orders to treat it as a single residence, the valuer must obey.

To be honest, the more you learn about the valuation, the more you get to know. So, there is more to understanding property valuation. Let's continue.

If you hadn't known before, understand that sales evidence has a lot to do with the valuation process. I'll be discussing it below along with the ways investors can benefit from the valuation process. You already know the famous saying that says a property is worth only if someone is paying to purchase it. But then, if the property has no improvements or is not being sold, how can the value be determined? How will the valuer do the valuation?

Well, this is when the sales evidence comes into the picture. For example, if there is a crime, you will be finding a reason for the crime with the help of the evidence. Hence, this is similar to such an incident. The valuer will focus on the sales of properties that are located in comparable areas.

The details gathered from the inspection, and the comparison of the target properties, will help the valuer to decide the valuation. If there are a lot of similarities between the compared and the target properties the accuracy of the valuation will increase too. Around 3 or more properties will be considered when handling sales evidence, and the sales must have happened recently, in the last few months. Nevertheless, in the changing market, the valuer might consider sales occurred within three months.

Along with the analysis done on the sales evidence, it is possible to write a report mentioning the properties compared and targeted and how they differ. The report will include the valuation, and it will be given to the one who requested a valuation. Assume, if the lender sought a valuation, then the borrower will not receive a copy of it. Yet, the borrower can request a valuation report.

The cost pressure and time are the significant barriers faced by the values. The valuation fee is low, hence, spending a lot of time on a single valuation will not be a wise move. Also, a valuer must struggle with legal pressures as well.

Anyway, are there any reasons why the investor has to understand the process of valuation? There are certain reasons:

By following the value of the property that investor can offer a right amount or avoid paying more than the required amount.

You will be able to get benefits for the new property or the current property based on the process of valuation.

- You will be able to make a steady case on a higher valuation.

- You can emphasize the positive points of the property.

- If you understand the valuer's duty, you will avoid patronizing them.

As an investor, you will be able to enjoy the above benefits. But then, what if you use an online tool for the property valuation? Will it be beneficial?

Nowadays, nothing is impossible if you have access to the internet. You will be able to learn everything at your comfort. You can learn everything that you need to know about real estate investment. However, you can find a lot of property valuation tools. If you want to pick one, you have to read reviews and check whether they are worth considering. So, once you find a property valuation tool, you can quickly get things done. But will you have the same satisfaction as doing it traditionally? Well, that is questionable. Yet, by reading the benefits and risks of online valuation tools, you can come to a conclusion whether it is reliable or not! Actually, it is evident that the internet has a lot of information needed for both parties. Hence, it is recommended to spend time and do some research. Anyway, I'll mention the benefits and risks that you must consider:

Benefits of considering online valuation tools

As a beginner, you might find this extremely beneficial. The online valuation tool is pretty easy and flexible. You just have to enter the data, and the tool will provide the value. However, this valuation should be considered a guide. You can show the valuation report to emphasize the amount that you can pay. Also, you can consider this as a reference tool.

Risks of considering online valuation tools

There will be different formulas used by different valuation tools so that valuation may differ slightly. This is the primary reason why online valuation tools should be considered a guide alone.

The results generated from the online valuation tool is automatic, and it will be based on the information that you enter. The last sales price and other data will not be taken into consideration; hence, it is better to hire a professional if you want the valuation report for other purposes than a guide. And I hope I have provided a sufficient amount of information based on property valuation.

Chapter 8: Guidelines to decide that you are selecting the right property

I know how it feels to buy a home. It is definitely exciting. I'm a person with an interest in hunting in the real estate market. If you are also like me, you would love to hunt because it gives you excitement. The entire process can be handled by a good agent who is well-versed in the real estate market. Apparently, the agent will have the in and out knowledge of the market.

The real estate market has developed a lot. It has become one of the top markets in the world. Because of the popularity, there is competitiveness in the market. Many agents and brokerages are there from which you have to pick the best. But the hardest part is to select the best agent or brokerage amongst the sea of choices. If you are lucky enough to get in touch with an experienced agent who is both reliable and skilled, you would be able to build a successful journey in the real estate market. Or you can find the best property at the best price.

However, it is not easy to find the right property in the real estate market; also, you are a naïve investor. Thus, things can become more robust. I will offer a few guidelines to select the right property. But before worrying about the property, you have to think about the real estate agent, right? So, I will mention a few tips that you must consider when hiring a real estate agent. Here are a few tips that you must utilize when hiring an agent:

Both experience and the person matter

Of course, you must not focus on the experience alone. Instead you must think about the individual as well. The agent that you hire must be of worth to you when handling real estate properties. If you think experience is the only factor that matters, you are wrong. Even a naïve agent can do a lot better than an experienced agent if he or she has the skill. You must consider the level of experience as well as the skills of the individual. To be honest, you must look for his or her character because you would be with the agent most of the time. He or she should be someone real and friendly. You must find someone who can talk and discuss real estate investment.

A good relationship is needed

If you are going to pick someone randomly, please, don't! I recommend interviewing a few agents before settling on a specific agent that you are going to work with. There are many factors to consider such as hyperlocal factor, neighborhood expertise, and most importantly, a good relationship builder. Make sure to look for these factors when you are selecting an agent.

Find referrals from homeowners

I know many would disagree with this tip, but trust me, human communication and human relationships are valuable. No matter the online websites that are available, you would always find a great agent through referrals from your human connection, i.e., homeowners. Referrals are still accessible and reliable. If you find an agent through referral, there is no second guess as to whether he or she is the right choice. In fact, a referral is one of the most significant compliments an agent could get. You can ask homeowners for a recommendation.

Someone with a real interest

An agent should have a genuine interest. He or she should think about you rather than being self-centered. If you want to find such an agent, you must be honest about your search. You must use a tricky question to check whether the agent has a real interest. Or if you have already hired and you are not feeling right, you don't have to ponder on it. Instead look for another agent who is genuinely interested in serving as an agent.

Sometimes let it to your guts

At times, it is better to let your gut feelings make the decisions. Right? Once the decision is made, you feel so right about doing it. Well, gut feeling is also created by your brain along with emotions. First of all, you must consider the agent's skills, past work, and other details. And then, second of all, listen to your guts. If you feel that you must hire him or her, just do it!

Trust is the pillar

When you are hiring an agent, you must bear in mind that trust is the pillar of a successful relationship in the real estate market. However, when interviewing you must listen to the agent while watching them closely. Look and study the way he or she converses. You have to look for a human being who understands your goals and aims and works accordingly to achieve it. A tech-savvy will find options for you, but will he or she be the agent that you are looking for? Well, NO! You must take time and decide because you will need the agent's support throughout the journey. Thus, trust is vital, so look for it!

Search for a passion-oriented person

You can easily say if a person is interested in his or her work by looking at his past work. Or if he or she is a newbie, you can understand it from their way of communicating. If the person is excited to discuss work, it means he or she is passion-oriented. You are looking for a person to help you find the right deals, so make sure he or she is ready for it.

Seek a supportive person

Do your homework. Do search about the agents that you have shortlisted. If the agent has a supportive team, it is a plus point. If there is a supportive team, it means better customer service. Actually, logistics related to investment isn't easy to understand. You can easily miss a few things, so the agent with a supportive team will have fewer chances of making such errors.

Factor of risk mitigation

I mentioned trust, but I did not mention honesty because I believe they interrelate. However, if you consider this tip you would have to focus on reliability. The agent that you work with must offer honest reviews and ideas. He or she must inform you of the risks related to the property that you have picked. Don't settle for flattery agents; it might feel good but is not worthy for investment business. The agent should mitigate risk while being realistic. Hence, when interviewing, you can shoot questions with hypothetical incidents. Then, based on their answers you can study them up to some extent.

Not without core values

Be it business or normal life, core values are something that you cannot live without. The agent will be playing your role so having core values count a lot. If you are an honest person, you won't tolerate a deceitful person. Thus, you cannot do without core values.

Compassion is crucial

You and I both know real estate investing is stressful even though it is profitable. Of course, you are new to the market, yet, by now, you would have some understanding about the real estate investment. Anyway, in such a market, you cannot handle your problems without the support of a compassionate agent. Let's say you have had a bad day at home, so with such a mindset you cannot focus on buying a property. In such a situation, the agent has to be patient while maintaining other things. So, when hiring an agent, you must look for the personality, idea, and the way of thinking.

Crystal-clear communication

This tip should be added to the top of the list because without good communication you cannot do anything in the real estate investment industry. However, when hiring an agent, you must find someone whom you can communicate with comfortably. For some reason, if you feel awkward communicating with your agent, then he or she is not the one for you. Keep searching until you find someone who you can communicate with.

Look for web information

I know, I mention about referrals while discouraging online search. But, what is right for you may not be right for another person. So, in such cases, web information might be helpful. You can Yelp or Google agents. You can search for more details once you shortlist a few choices. You can even look for their websites. Use the available sources to find the right agent.

Finally, the long list of tips has come to an end. You already know that buying a property is time-consuming, costly, and complicated. These three things are the main reason why sellers and buyers look for help from agents. They want agents to help them throughout the investment journey. The agent will handle a lot of issues that come along. Most of the time, it is the agent who handles the buying process whereas the actual buyer does it a few times only. But, then, you would ask why you can't directly contact the agent. Well, there is a reason, i.e., time. The agent will do the paperwork, coordinating with relevant authorities, and many other activities that are otherwise to be done by the buyer. So, you get my point?

Anyway, that was about finding an agent. Without an agent, buying a property would be a tough deal. But there is more that you need to learn about buying a property. Let me help you!

Although I said about selecting an agent which is a significant factor when buying a property, there are some other guidelines that you must know. Generally, an excellent property can enhance your wealth with time. But, if you don't pick the right property, it will be an unattainable dream. Also, if you make a mistake when selecting a property, it will cost you financially as well as mentality. As you are a beginner, you will have a lot of hopes about the market. So, if it goes wrong or if it continually happens, you might even quit investing. Thus, it is essential to get things right as much as possible. The setbacks in real estate investment can create headache and stress. You would be able to set those setbacks at bay if you follow these guidelines when purchasing a property. Let's read.

Capital growth – This is one of the essential guidelines when purchasing a property. You must always consider capital growth. In simple terms, you must look for areas that expand in population, infrastructure, economy, and many other capital growth-related factors.

A known location – Well, now, don't ask me whether you need to invest in your backyard (pun-intended). This means, once you have selected an investment property, you must get to know the area or the location. You must search for it. Try to get to know the neighborhood. Research it your best, look for vacancy rates, capital growth rate, demographic detail, and much more.

Focus on returns – If you don't have a good cash flow, or if it is tight, you must be considerate about the property that you buy. It shouldn't worsen your situation. So, make sure to think about the rental yield before making a decision.

Follow up the future – When you are considering a property you must follow up the future of that area. You can look for council websites and government information to get details on the planned infrastructure projects. Or you can contact the council to get details. However, this guideline generally means that you must look for developments in the area that you are investing in. For example, shopping hubs, schools, or any other amenities that will increase the value of the property.

Low maintenance or hire a service provider – If you don't have bigger plans like flipping and fixing properties, you must find a property that has a low requirement for maintenance. Or better, hire a service provider to do the needful.

Study the tenants – Before you settle on a decision you must research. You must study the tenants in that area to find their demands. If you find the demand of the larger group, you will be able to cater to their needs through which you can make a good income. For example, if you find a single-family property at a lower rate and then if you don't find tenants who are in need of single-family property, wouldn't that be a loss? So, make sure to know the market before deciding anything.

Selecting an ideal investment property will need high-end research and a great study up. You must try to gather as much information as you can. It is much better if you can talk to a few experienced investors and professionals in the real estate industry. Researching, learning, and seeking should never end!

Also, these tips will help you when you are trying to find the right property. Let's read!

Mind vs. Heart

Will you allow your heart to decide or the brain to decide? It is advisable to stick to your mind. In fact, you may like a place, but you should consider the facilities of the surrounding area, and its advantages. Ask yourself, will this place have a good market? Will it grab the attention of the clients? If you find definite answers for the issue, then you can carry on with the purchase, but when you don't see it as the correct place then don't allow the heart decide. At the end you should have a profit, not a loss.

Don't compromise on planning

Most failures occur when the investors are lacking plans. But remember, if you want to achieve the target you should set up goals. And just creating goals is not enough; you should start working toward it. You should find out the type of home you need to purchase, and then find out if it will meet the expectations of the clients. By doing this you have a low-risk of falling into the wrong place.

PATIENCE.PATIENCE.PATIENCE.

Patience may seem like a small word but it decides the future, "I can be a millionaire with just one padding night" thoughts of some investors. They just think only about the tremendous amount of money and fail to concentrate on the hard work. It is advisable to maintain patience and slowly you will find yourself going in the direction of success. Wait until the rate of properties rise, and then enter the deal, instead of joining the agreement to make quick money.

Not learning enough

You may think one look at the sites and books are enough to gain success, but it is not. You should often stick to tips and information regarding the real estate career, in fact, it is a good idea if you take notes on the tips. You should always be in touch with learning if you want to succeed in real estate.

Hence, with these above tips and guidelines, you will be able to select the right property. So, think about the success you will face, though you will have to cross many hurdles and break many barriers. The hardships are worth the try!

Chapter 9: Key points to decide a good and a bad deal

No matter how well-versed you are with the investment. Even if you know the pros and cons of the investment, there is no point if you cannot find a good and a bad deal. Also, none of the investors prefer a terrible deal. Of course, price is important but finding a property without wasting your time and effort can be tough. However, it is not easy to identify the problem with the property if you are not hawk-eyed about it. If you want to find a good deal, there are certain factors that you must consider. And here are some:

Location is the concern

If you want to find the right deals, you must bear this factor in mind. Unless the location is excellent, you wouldn't be able to make a good income. A good deal is defined when you can make a steady income from it. A great location is when there is a high inflow of visitors. Only if you have a steady flow of visitors will you be able to make a steady income.

Consider off-market properties

Some landlords consider shopping around in a quiet way rather than public listing. Through this method, the current tenants are not being disturbed. So, the investors who are new to the market should not wait until the homeowners or property owners find them; instead, the investors should find the property owners.

Possible tear-down

Most real estates don't understand the value of overpriced, run-down, small homes within a specific city limit. You can sell this home to a developer. Then, larger homes can reach more benefits with zoning permits. In order to enter into such deals, you need good vision and faith that it will work. However, you will face obstacles when you are dealing with this kind of deal.

Don't run away from smelly homes

You shouldn't run away from smelly homes. There wouldn't be competition for these homes, so you wouldn't have to compete. You just have to invest in a stinky house. Then, pay to fix them, and then it will be ready to rent out. Even though you have to focus on repairing and renovating, this type of deal is excellent.

Look for properties outside the state

If you are interested in investing outside the area that you are residing in, you can, of course, go for it. You can purchase outside the state or the city. But, when you are buying outside the state, you must make sure to consider the neighborhood of the property. You must not overlook the factor of educating yourself before you invest in this type of investment. Also, you must not forget to hire a management company to do the needful.

However, these are not the *only* points that you must consider when securing a good deal, but these are the *key* points that you must consider.

However, there are some tips that you need to know when you are dealing with real estate investment. Shall we have a look at those?

1. Connect with people

When you are in the real estate market you connect with people, and when you connect, the network widens. The wider the network, the higher the engagement. You will be able to become successful along with the connections that you connect to. You must try to build more and more relationships in the investment market. However, it doesn't happen overnight, rather you will have to work for it.

2. Focus on your property

As you have studied, financing the property that you are going to live in easy. You will be able to reside in home while writing-off tax. Then, you can move into a better house after some time. So, you have to repeat the procedure, but make sure to rent out the first property.

3. Be focused about expenses

You must not overlook the expenses, mainly, when you purchase single-family properties. There can be hidden costs which might impact your profit. Also, you have to deal with maintenance costs that must be handled by the owner.

4. The market has a power

If you think that the market is powerless, you are wrong. You might be handling a type of investment, but the market will move as per its needs. Hence, you must think about the power of the market if you don't want to face sudden challenges.

5. Fair expectations

You must know where you stand. You must know the reason why you are trading. You must bear in mind that there are pro factors, yet it doesn't mean you will make quick income. Hence, your expectations must be reasonable.

6. *Don't overcomplicate it*

Most naïve investors assume that real estate is complicated, but it is not. This is an easy market. It wouldn't be complicated unless you complicate it. Of course, there can be times when you have to let your instincts make the decisions. But, you must not try to automate the analysis as it can create a sophisticated environment for investing. Hence, like the famous K.I.S.S. strategy in trading, keep it simple, stupid!

7. *Leveraging is not an 'oh-so-good'*

Nowadays, naïve investors consider leveraging as one of the best methods of financing when they want to purchase a property. Well, it is not the best. In fact, you might be in a risky situation once you consider leveraging. You must get away from the myth of leveraging. Of course, you can make money without being indebted to anyone. If you don't have enough money to begin your investment journey, remain patient, until you get the money that you need. Waiting is much better than taking up a risk like leveraging.

8. *Your strength is your power*

There are many people who don't treat their strength as a powerful factor. They try a certain investment type and then move to another. Likewise, they keep moving when someone else recommends it without being confident about what they do. Why does it happen? Well, if you like wholesaling, don't think too much about whether you will do it well or not. Take some time. Learn about it. Be focused on wholesaling and try to collect as much insight as possible. Don't keep moving from one to another. Instead stay focused on a particular investment. Specialize in it because you can do a lot better than you think! No matter the type that you have selected, become a maestro at it!

9. *Flexibility is cool*

You already know that this is a dynamic sector. If you don't have experience related to investment, look for other ways to enhance knowledge. You must make an effort to get the complete understanding of the types of investment.

Luckily, you can find information on a few investment types in this guide. Also, you must be flexible because you are not going spend your life in the investment industry, rather you might have other commitments as well. You must be flexible and the real estate will automatically adapt.

10.Spread the 'trust' basement

This doesn't mean you have to work with family and friends. The ones whom you connect with, examples such as banker, broker, developer, contractor, and investor, must be reliable and professional. In real estate, relationships with your network plays a huge role.

11.Perseverance is perfection

When you rush into a decision, they are likely to go wrong. In fact, when you rush you might even sign a deal that seems too impeccable. Do you want to do such mistakes in this market? Let alone the risks, you have just started your journey. If you rush into a decision you will end up giving up on real estate investment. However, if you are patient your reward will be huge!

12.Market cycles are vital

You might be a beginner, but you are not the exception when dealing with market cycles. When you are in a cyclical market your excitements can be at the top, but control! Of course, you wouldn't find a market that doesn't create the hype, so being vigilant is important. You must research before you make any decision. This tip applies even when you become an experienced investor.

Sometimes, we tend to ignore the simple things. But there are situations in life when those simple things have a higher impact. Similarly, in the real estate market, you will come across simple things and you might just shoo it away assuming that it wouldn't impact your decision. But, you are wrong! Even a small piece of information can help you in decision making. Real estate deals with a lot of information and practical ideas, hence, you must focus on those. Meanwhile, I have provided a few tips that can benefit you now and in the future.

Chapter 10: Mistakes made by real estate investors

I think this is an essential topic that needs to be covered because most investors enter the market without the awareness of the market and they end up failing. If you don't want to fail like other naïve investors, you must consider the following mistakes that are often faced. Also, remember, facing mistakes is a common thing that happens in every market so you must not be discouraged reading these mistakes. But you must be discouraged if you are repeating the mistakes over and over. Hence, try to read and understand these mistakes to avoid them in the long run. Let's begin!

Unreasonable payment

Being considerate about the investment type is not enough if you are making an unreasonable payment. For example, you might purchase a property that doesn't have enough amenities, yet you will be paying an amount that is not worth paying. A naïve investor usually experiences this. I think, this mistake often repeats due to not understanding the ways to secure a deal. But it cannot be the only reason; sometimes, you might be hyped about being in the real estate sector. A lot of naïve investors make huge mistakes due to the excitement of entering the market. What can you do to avoid these mistakes? Well, once you enter the market, don't try to secure any deals even if it comes your way (but this is a rarity!). Anyway, wait for some time. Move around and see the market. Take time to understand and research the market. Once your excitement reduces, think about entering into deals. If you do so, you will be able to control yourself from making unreasonable payments.

Not understanding the market

You must have an understanding about the task that you are engaged in. The understanding should be perfect. If not, you are likely to be fooled. This strategy applies in real estate too.

Without a clear understanding of the background and the entire market, you will have a hard time in the market. You wouldn't be able to make a good deal. You wouldn't be able to find a good client. And moreover, you wouldn't be able to make a profit. To avoid all these, you must make an effort to learn the market. With the help of technology, you can easily find a wide range of sources to study the real estate market.

Inability to gain due diligence

Lack of attention is another factor which creates disappointment. Due to lack of awareness, you might miss out a lot of important points. You should try many methods to invest and alternative plans so that you can stay away from the mistakes. If you don't have due diligence, it is no wonder that you are struggling. As an investor, it is a must to gain due diligence otherwise it is impossible to become a successful investor. This mistake commonly occurs when you are heedless. But, you do not have to be like other naïve investors, you can focus on the overall market and try to improve your due diligence to perform better in the market.

Making decisions in a rush

A decision taken in a hurry will lead to disappointment; if it happens in real estate, then it is a huge mistake as you have invested a significant amount. Just jumping into a conclusion without focusing on the neighborhood, rents, and values will lead to a considerable loss. Rather than investing your money in vain, you must invest your time in learning the property. A rushed decision will often happen when the investor finds good deals. Even though deals are right, you must not make rushed decisions because you wouldn't allocate time to consider the critical factors. Actually, there are a lot of steps in purchasing a property; even the steps will differ based on the type of the property. Hence, you must not make decisions without considering all these steps and tips.

Not sticking to a budget

Budgeting is the key to the thriving real estate market. It is understandable that a naïve investor will struggle to control emotions. But, it is never an impossible task. Through practice and patience, you will be able to control your emotions. However, one of the common mistakes related to emotions is budgeting. Most investors enter into a contract or purchase a property without deciding on a budget. They make decisions out of excitement; hence, it is evident that they make mistakes. They don't think about the property price because they are overly excited that they got a deal. Yet, this is not a healthy move in real estate. So, by controlling emotions, you can stay within the budget and minimize the errors.

Trying out illegal signs

Well, this is not a mistake, more an endpoint to your investment journey. You have just entered the investment journey. Do you want to handle illegal signs? If yes, you're not going to make it THAT far in the real estate investment world.

Slow earning is better than a rapid income through illegal activities. Hence, you must understand not to turn to the illegal side; rather try to make good money with the help of guides, articles, and many other great sources. Also, you must not make this mistake when you are investing.

Confusing on speculating vs. investing

Just theorizing the ideas by considering the future is a negative effect; it is great to look towards the future market but is it only through theory without exerting any effort? If you think so, then, you are wrong. You must make sure to dedicate your time and effort in whatever you do include real estate investment. Just reading, learning, and understanding the market will not do any good. You must prepare yourself to face the consequences.

Not understanding the exact cost

This is a huge mistake made by investors. You invest an amount on the property with a lack of facilities such as parking and a street packed with a huge crowd. Finally, you invest a huge amount in a property that isn't worth the pay and then to add those prime facilities you have to put in an extra amount which will eventually disfavor you. Also, as an investor, you must make sure you understand the exact cost or at least the average cost. If you don't understand the cost, you wouldn't be able to reach the ultimate profit target. In fact, not understanding the cost will make the investor charge a lower amount than the amount the property deserves. This is a huge loss that a naïve investor must avoid as much as possible.

Falling for the beauty

Investors should have control over their emotions especially if you are naïve. Selecting a building with a lavish kitchen top but with a small parking lot can be the insane decision that you make. Sometimes, it might become a habit to select the more beautiful property than the more valuable property. If it happens, you wouldn't be able to remain in the market for a long time. Hence, you must not fall for beauty, but rather check for available facilities and advantages in a property when making a decision. It can be tough if you have the habit of liking beautiful properties, but before you enter the market, you must educate yourself about this factor. Also, you must work on correcting the mistakes if you feel that you are making any of these mistakes.

Losing the humanity

It is not only the properties which you should be concerned about but also the people. Even though you are naïve, you are a human so you must have the humanity in you. So, when making a deal or buying a property, you must not lose the humanity in you. You must have core values when you are in the real estate investment world. Of course, there is no one to control you, but that doesn't mean you have to give up on core values. You must adhere to core values Only then can you achieve a lot in this investment journey.

Not having a good team

Teamwork plus hard work creates successes: some investors in real estate have bad team cooperation which will lead the whole team to failed missions. It will also have a negative impact on the clients who prefer to have deals with you. A right team is essential as real estate needs loads of research and knowledge regarding the project they work in. So by choosing the right team, you will have a positive impact and a future. This mistake shouldn't be repeated. If you cannot find a team at the very beginning, try to create a team. You must always have faith that you can create a good team to support you. Of course, as a beginner, you cannot do it right away. But with time, you will end up teaming up with a bunch of great people.

Collect funds internally

As naïve investors, you will have a hard time to gain finance so you may decide to ask your friends and family. But this is a mistake because you will end up becoming a debtor. Do you want to generate income by being a debtor? I advise getting some ideas and tips from a professional or an advisor who are well-versed in the real estate market. Actually, there are a lot of methods that you can consider when you are looking for a method to finance your property. So, why become a debtor?

The easy decision is not the right decision

This is a dangerous mistake many naïve investors make, as it is said every penny counts in business. It may seem easy to go for a low-cost option, but the results may be dangerous so always try to think about the results before jumping into the final decision. Most naïve investors try to opt for easy decisions, and I don't think it is wise to make such decisions. If you are being lured towards ease, it means you are not ready to take challenges. You are not ready to work hard. But, real estate is not a simple business until you become a pro. If you are a beginner, you would have to do a lot to remain in this market. Let alone remain. An investor wouldn't be able to secure good deals if the focus is on the easy road. Try to stay away from the myth of considering easy deals.

Not getting help from a good broker

Brokers' experiences are the key. A naïve investor's support pillar is the broker so you shouldn't think twice to get the support of an experienced broker. Yet, most naïve investors don't focus on the experience, but they do hire a broker for the sake of it. But, you shouldn't make that mistake. When you are hiring a broker, be sure to consider the experience level of the broker. Hence, the broker will help you with situations such as an eye for many buildings in one attempt, purchasing properties from inexperienced sellers, inadequate information on daily income, and an experienced broker will seek more things. So, the main work you should do is to find a broker with experience in real estate investment. It is not hard because there are many websites and other sources through which you will be able to find the right broker.

Not striving to succeed

Naïve investors tend to face the problem of giving up. There are many reasons for these thoughts such as financial shortage, interfering with a well-known business tycoon, stress and frustration, illegal activities, and rules and regulations. But you should not put all these facts in front to distract your success. For a naïve investor, the hurdles may urge you to give up, but you should not turn away by looking at the hurdles. Instead cross them and stay strong. There will be a few challenges when you are starting your investment journey, but over time you will learn to handle the challenges. Until you become well-versed, you have to keep moving forward.

Unclear communication leads to failure

Communication is the tool that connects you with buyers, investors, realtors, and all the other professionals. Hence, it is important to communicate clearly and nicely. Also, being aggressive with professionals in the real estate market will not be a good solution. As naïve investors, you must try to connect with the right parties by communicating in the right manner. I agree, at first, it can be pretty tough to communicate with the agents, brokers, and other professionals. But, once you manage a few deals, you will be comfortable.

Not being an honest person

Trust is very important in business, as it is the brick to build a strong relationship. Trust is mainly broken when you overstate things. This can often happen in the real estate market because you aim to sell the property. But, if you are not honest about your deals and properties, you will not be able to remain in the market for a long time. So, it is better not to overstate things, rather tell it as it is. This is why you must invest by considering all the factors, or when buying a property, you must be vigilant. If you do so, you don't have to lie to the buyer. Also, most naïve investors with the aim of making a quick income tend to overstate things to make money, but do you think it will bring them success? This is not a market that can be controlled, so you shouldn't try to do it!

Don't become one of them

Uniqueness is important in a competitive market. You should not just do what other investors do instead of trying something new, which will grab the attention of buyers. Being creative is not restricted to the real estate market. Also, sometimes, following others may become the reason why you would be kicked out of the market. So, you have the liberty to do creative things, why not give it a try? Don't repeat the mistakes that other traders made!

Being irresponsible

When you are dealing with a client or a buyer, you must be responsible. So you should be available when there is a conversation regarding the investment, or you should at least inform them beforehand. As naïve investors remember to be available to your clients. You can even attract clients by being a responsible individual. Actually, responsibility is important to gain good deals and great income.

As you already know so much about the market, it is pointless to repeat. Similarly, as you already know the mistakes that a naïve investor might make, you must stay away from it. It is better if you can learn more errors that are caused by other investors so that you won't do it in your investment journey. Try not to make mistakes, but it doesn't mean that you will never make a mistake. You are a human so mistakes can happen. Just don't repeat them!

Chapter 11: Why should you start a real estate world

Choosing a real estate business can be a good idea. Even though you are naïve to this, you will face failures, but you can figure out mistakes and correct them. Although real estate seems easy, it also needs hard work: as the saying goes 'hard-works pays off.' This applies when selecting this investment journey. But, before you jump into the real estate world, it is advisable to check out some information related to entering the real estate world. You will find a lot of insights in this chapter. If you focus on it you can quickly get an answer to your question, "Why should I enter the real estate world?"

Before I move on, let me tell you it is not at all easy to find an excellent income-generating method, hence, when you do, you must hold onto it tight. For example, most people love to enter real estate, but not everybody gets to remain in the market. This is not about having or not having the skills. Anybody can become an investor through learning and hard work. But only a few will be able to remain consistent even if the market has ups and downs. However, if you want to stay consistent in the real estate world, you must focus on the reason why you entered the real estate market. When you know the reason it boosts your energy, and it makes you strive harder to become better at what you are doing! Without further ado, let me give you some insights on why you should be there in the real estate world.

It is not about being sales-y

You will master your skills as a real estate starter by dealing positively with the clients who come to you with the help of finding a solution to their real estate problems. You must be able to satisfy them with the skills of communicating and most importantly understanding their taste in the selection of property. You must develop these skills, but it doesn't mean that you have to be sales-y. It wouldn't take long to master these skills. So, this market is simple to enter, and it can be one of the reasons why you must remain in the real estate market.

Create a positive mindset

If you think why you should be in the real estate world, there are a lot of reasons. But the main reason is it helps to create a positive mindset. You wouldn't be discouraged just by one or two bad deals because there are a lot of investment groups that you can sign up to. If you are in those groups, you will be able to discuss with other members regarding the risks and hardships that you face. And you will be provided with tips and guidance. Also, you will be able to find a lot of books that are written on creating a positive mindset. Try to read them. If you want to remain in this great market, you must develop a positive mindset, and it is not! You must enter real estate and try out a few deals and accept the fact that this is not a tough market.

Have a simple, yet powerful plan

Small and big things pile up to form a successful investor, but the important fact is to start your investing journey with a proper plan which is the key to success. As a naïve real estate investor you should be able to handle clients methodically and always remember to stick to a plan before proceeding. Anybody can do this if they have a plan. Basically, you can remain in this market if you have a plan. But this applies to almost all markets. If you have a good plan, you are unlikely to go on the wrong track. Plus, I have explained a few points about goal-setting, so try to utilize those to create a great plan. Also, remember, giving up shouldn't be a choice once you enter the real estate market.

Know your budget

A budget is an essential factor in any business as it will have a great impact on every minute detail of the work you do. Make sure to start organizing a spreadsheet to summarize the expenditures which you do. Keep in mind to add the least cost in the list too. As from the small things begin the big things. It is not enough just budgeting. You should make it a habit of revising the summary so that you will get an idea to process further. You can do this in an excellent way when you are in the real estate world. So, there is no reason why you must stay away.

Welcome changes, it's natural

Changes occur with time. It is in our hands to adjust to the changes. Even in this real estate market you will face many changes but remind yourself to go with the changes, as doing so will lead you to success as a real estate investor. You are not the one who controls the market, but you can control your deals and selection. As there is flexibility in your journey, you don't have to worry. It is not like you are going to lose the entire investment when there is a tiny change. Hence, you must consider this factor to understand the reason why you must be in the market.

Stay away from assumptions

The majority of naïve people fail at the beginning of the journey of investment by assuming rather than engaging in real work; you should be an exception to that list. It is a negative mark if you assume without adding any hard work from your side. For example, as you have succeeded in earning from a new income source on your own it doesn't mean that your family and friends should refer to the real estate business, it is just an assumption. Instead, you should try to find out many clients and make them believe you by giving the positive impact about the real estate investment journey. Remember never jump into any conclusions before you know the whole scenario. Thus, by figuring out the positives and negatives, you will find out that by hard work and dedication you can succeed as a real estate investor. You can try out a few investments without losing a lot. Hence, you do not have to assume and work when you are in the real estate world.

Enjoy the liberty

One of the advantages of being in a real estate career is that you own, you set the time and duration according to the preference, and if by any chance you feel it hard to move out of your cozy home you can stay and work from home. This is one of the major reasons why you must enter the real estate market. I know how hard it is to follow the 9-5 job schedule. But that doesn't mean you have to give up on your day job. Of course, you can give up on your day job, but it shouldn't be done when you are a beginner in the real estate market. Rather, wait for the right time and conquer the market. If you feel that you will be able to make a steady income from this market, you can go for it and quit your day job. Whatever it is, the liberty in the real estate market is something enjoyable and appreciable.

Real estate is a quick start

A real estate career can be easily achieved by rapid progress; unlike other careers, you need not wait for a long time to build up a firm background in this real estate career. Some people still dream about becoming a professional real estate investor while others would have walked the path of success. It is mainly taking the initial step. You must not sit back and wait, rather you must try. So, this is not a market that restricts your entry, rather it welcomes you. To enter this market, you don't have to follow a lot of procedures; it is simple and easy. You can begin your journey without much effort. But, you have to work hard if you want to succeed.

Potential to earn some income

You can never guarantee a certain income in this real estate career as it depends on the growth of your business. Some people think that real estate is something which will eventually make you rich overnight, but this isn't the fact. You should not stick to the concept of quick money, but you should take all the steps with utmost care to become a successful investor. This will not happen if you are expecting quick income. The reason why you must enter this market is you have the potential to earn income even though it might not be quick. The strategies and techniques will decide how soon you will make income from the properties that you invest in.

Professionals help when in need

Choosing real estate is not just about the career. It is about the great work you do as an advisor, mentor, and supporter to find your client's dream house. For example, some families will find it hard to figure out the best houses or apartments to their beloved members in this situation; you will be the advisor to them. Not only families, even bachelors who wish to spend some quality time in a peaceful environment will struggle to select a building for them, so a professional like you can help them when they are in need. But this will not happen immediately. You have to become an experienced person by being consistent in real estate investment. This is nice because you will feel great about helping someone when they are in need. There are many jobs, and income-generating sources, but not every income-generating source or job has this great advantage.

Ability to become a pro

After you have been experiencing the real estate career, you will be an expert in the field. You will have a huge clientele base. Real estate also teaches you to progress yourself with the hard work and enthusiasm to achieve the goal. It is not only about making money but is also about learning. From your end, you must focus on providing the best. You must think about improving your skills. And your focus should be to become a professional real estate investor. If you don't have the aim to become a professional, then, no matter what the market offers, you will not utilize it efficiently.

Different financing options

This option is useful as you do not have to start your career by falling into a huge amount of debt or investing millions of penny with a doubt about your potential career; thus, you can utilize the leasing option or some other similar options available in the market. Leasing option will provide benefit when the market price is quite low you can purchase the apartment and then you could sell it to another at a profit. However, there are many such financing methods in the market. You shouldn't pick a financing option just because someone recommends it; rather, you must do your homework. As there are a lot of options available in the market, you can always research the type that you are planning to consider. When you research, you will find the pros and cons in considering a particular investment, and it will help you to make a good decision.

Well, why should you enter the real estate world? To conclude all these points, I'd say to make an extra income! Or you are looking for a career change. The reason why YOU enter will be different from another investor's reason. Hence, it is pretty tough to mention the reason why an investor should enter the real estate world. But, no matter why you are entering the real estate world, it is going to be an exciting journey! You have to dedicate your time, passion, and dedication to real estate to make it a reliable income source. Why wait? Give it a try!

Conclusion

Real estate investing is a path that opens up many other opportunities. If you are lagging out of fear, it will be at the cost of success. Do you want to give up on progress and good income? You wouldn't want it! Hence, you must garner all the possible information from this guide and utilize it in your investing journey.

The beginning has never been, so it is not going to be easy for you as well. As a naïve investor, you must focus on the basics. You must try to master the basics. Once you do, the rest will fall into place. Also, you shouldn't forget to keep learning because the more you learn, the better it becomes.

Even though you will be able to cover a lot from this book, it is always recommended to keep hunting for more information and knowledge. As I said, everything will be hard in the beginning, but once you get the grip, you can flaunt success.

Learning real estate can be like learning a new language for some people, but we never knew how to speak when we grew up, but then practice happened. Hence, training, learning, and experience will help you become a better investor. You have to focus on the learning procedure of investing and, eventually, you will master it!

I hope Real Estate Investing for Beginners Like You is nothing but great for you. I've covered a lot of sections that a naïve investor will need. Hope you are benefitted.

Kudos to successful investing!

www.ingramcontent.com/pod-product-compliance
Lightning Source LLC
Chambersburg PA
CBHW020846210326
41597CB00041B/871